WORKING WOMEN, WORKABLE LIVES

Creative Solutions for Managing Home and Career

WORKING WOMEN,

WORKABLE LIVES

Creative
Solutions for
Managing Home
and Career

Karen Scalf Linamen & Linda Holland

Harold Shaw Publishers
Wheaton, Illinois

ISBN 0-87788-851-5

Cover design by David LaPlaca

Library of Congress Cataloging-in-Publication Data

Linamen, Karen Scalf, 1960-
    Working women, workable lives : creative solutions for
managing home and career / Karen Scalf Linamen and
Linda Holland.
        p.   cm.
    ISBN 0-87788-851-5
    1. Working mothers—United States.   2. Work and family—
United States.   I. Holland, Linda, 1948-   . II. Title.
HQ759.48.L58   1993
640'.240431—dc20   93-15998
                                                         CIP

99 98 97 96 95

10 9 8 7 6 5 4 3 2

To Kaitlyn Rose, with the prayer
that by the time you're old enough
to really think about these issues,
our generation will have managed
to work out a few of the bugs.

And to Larry.
Behind every successful working woman . . .
there should be someone as wonderful as you.

Love,
Karen

To Tami, now a mother also,
with the hope that every season of your life—
though each vastly different from the others—
will brim with joy and challenge,
opportunity and love.

And to Chris and Dallas
who continue to bring me great joy
as sons and as friends.

Love,
Linda

CONTENTS

Developing Wholeness As a Person

Developing Wholeness As a Family

Creative Problem Solving

Foreword

Once upon a time, not so very long ago, I had a dream that I would live a life of perfect balance. Of course I would have a wonderful career and would rapidly rise to the top of my chosen profession. And I would have children, too. They would be cute and obedient and live life on schedule. I would effortlessly manage these two aspects of my life without so much as chipping my nail polish.

I last wore nail polish in 1982. I remember the occasion—I was in the early stages of labor and was applying polish so I would look well-groomed in the delivery room photo. If that explains a little about my view of motherhood, I can only tell you that life has been an ongoing series of negotiations between reality and fantasy ever since.

I have been reminded daily of the realities: a son who tells me that he needs a costume for the school play the day before his acting debut; another son who can break out of any lock I place on the door and be down the block before I know he's gone; a career so chaotic that one time, while boarding a flight to Denver, I handed the flight attendant a parking ticket instead of my boarding pass!

The fantasies occur less in my mind and more often in the articles I read or the television shows that portray working mothers who never break into a sweat. There are just too many days when I look at these fantasy portrayals and wonder, *Am I the only woman who struggles?*

That's why I laughed and cried and called a half dozen friends when I read *Working Women, Workable Lives*. This was the first time that someone understood what it is *really* like to be a woman who loves her husband and kids, likes her job, and often wonders if she is selfish or crazy to try to do it all.

I love the practical nature of this book as well as the sympathetic tone, which helps me feel understood. After reading these pages I feel as if I am part of a sorority of Christian working women instead of the *only* woman in the world who reads her Bible while sitting in the carpool line at school, only to be interrupted by a call on her car phone from the office.

Somehow I know that the authors understand this crazy life. And since you're reading this book maybe you do too. That makes me feel hopeful. And it makes me realize that we all need to help each other as we stumble along. I'm grateful to Linda and Karen for doing that for me and the many other women who will read this wonderful book.

—Dale Hanson Bourke

Acknowledgments

Without making this page akin to a night at the Oscars, we nevertheless owe a great debt of gratitude to a number of people.

Harold Shaw, of course, deserves our heartfelt thanks for supporting us with an enthusiastic and brilliant staff . . . for believing enough in this book to give it this shot . . . and for sharing our concern over the many complex issues facing women of the 1990s.

We also want to thank Dr. H. Norman Wright for the generous hours he invested with us, shedding light on a great many issues examined in this book. Drs. Ralph Ricco, Keith Edwards, Cherry Steinmeier, and Anita Sorenson also provided countless and valuable perspectives from their professional and personal lives. Paula Star and the Ventura County Professional Women's Network contributed time and insights that deserve our recognition as well.

Many special thanks go to George and Nancy Barna. Their generous guidance helped us gather input from hundreds of working women, while discussion with Nancy helped formulate some of the ideas in this book.

We'd also like to thank Sylvia Nash and Judy Stewart, M.A. Their candid observations have been invaluable, adding depth (as well as a previously unplanned chapter!).

Finally, our sincere gratitude goes to the hundreds of women who took part in our survey, and the dozens more who have shared candid stories of their battle scars and victories as working women. Many of their stories appear throughout the following pages, and, in a very real sense, this is their book.

Any similarity between the authors and the stressed-out, over-worked, and harried examples with which they are connected in this book is, let's face it, totally accurate. In other cases, the names are changed to protect the guilty, not the innocent—the actual situations are far too real!

DEVELOPING WHOLENESS AS A PERSON

Betty Friedan said I can have it all.
The only question now is, can I take it?

1

The Myth
of Superwoman

Where Did Superwoman Come From . . .
and How Can We Send Her Back?

I spotted The Greeting Card while standing in aisle number six of my local supermarket. My daughter, who was at that time three years old, was wrestling with a box of animal crackers (her weekly shopping bribe), so I actually had several undistracted seconds in which to read the card.

The cover featured a cartoon mother in a business suit, just home from the office after an obviously wrenching day. Droopy-eyed and limp-lipped, she lay draped over an easy chair, just beneath the caption:

> We women can do it all!
> Ambition drives us forward.
> Common sense gives us direction.
> Experience gives us perspective.

I opened the card for the punch line:

> ... and bone-crushing fatigue
> kind of pulls it all together.

I laughed so hysterically that a blue-haired old lady pushing a cartload of cat food teetered up and asked if I needed a hand getting to the check-out.

I shook my head, grabbed one—no, two—cards, and wheeled my way toward the lane marked "Oversized Load." (It's especially popular with working moms who are too worn out to shop for food until their kids begin demanding real milk again with their Cheerios instead of Cremora).

While unloading my groceries and batting Kaitlyn's hands away from the gum rack, I fought an overwhelming urge to go back to aisle six and buy every droopy-eyed, limp-lipped cartoon woman I could find. I wanted to keep a card for myself, of course. And the second card was for a friend named Robyn. Yet the more I thought about it, the list of friends who deserved this card continued to grow:

- **Robyn,** mother of two, recently went back to work full-time after a downturn in her husband's sales volume caused a glitch in their budget.

- **Jenny,** a new mom, runs a home day care to supplement her husband, Jeff's, income as a Christian musician and songwriter.

- **Melita** has worked at a bank, in loan applications, ever since her husband walked out on her six years ago. She's raising their sixteen-year-old daughter alone.

- **Christine's** full-time job at a hospital meets her need to minister outside the home, yet it's still a juggling act to keep up with husband, Dan, and three preteens at home.

■ **Ann,** expecting her second baby, is an executive at the advertising firm where she works full-time.

Linda Holland deserves a card as well. In addition to cowriting this book with me, she holds down a demanding editorial position at a publishing house while single-parenting her family.

As for me, I began working at home six years ago, alternately jiggling a baby on my lap and meeting free-lance writing deadlines. I thought I had the perfect system until a client asked me about the pabulum on an invoice I submitted.

No two stories are alike. Yet each of these women knows what it's like to "have it all":

- the job
- the home
- the family
- and the burnout, stress, and guilt that comes with being . . .
  (drum roll, please)
  Superwoman.

You know who she is. She's touted on TV commercials and in magazine articles and in the company newsletter for her most recent contribution to her department. She's the woman in high heels, buying TV dinners in the freezer section. She's the one balancing a portfolio in one hand and Huggies in the other, planning a strategy meeting while taking her turn at the car-pool.

Did you see the movie *Superman* (what number?) with heartthrob Christopher Reeves? For three-quarters of the movie, our handsome hero manages to report the news, save the world, and woo the girl without breaking into a sweat. He corks a volcano, rounds up nuclear missiles in space, addresses an assembly of the United Nations—and his curl never unfurls.

But after a grueling battle with a solar-powered nemesis, Superman retreats to nurse his wounds. Lois Lane finds him in his Clark Kent apartment, shivering beneath a blanket in a darkened room. Pale, weak, and drenched with sweat, our hero is dying.

Even Superman has limits.

In the movie, the comic book hero recuperates and goes on to save the world—again. But in real life, millions of American working women—each juggling two worlds of her own—aren't so lucky. And many of these women may find themselves more quickly identifying with a shattered, broken Superperson than with the indefatigable Superhero.

Author Elsa Houtz put it this way:

> I had it all—job, home, family—so why did I feel like I was losing my mind? I was an intelligent, capable person, a successful executive who managed a large department efficiently. Why couldn't I manage my life better? Everything in my world was nice—nice house, nice child, nice husband, nice job, nice friends—but something inside me was not nice at all. Inside I was lonely, bruised and hurting.[1]

Perhaps it's time we sent Superwoman back to the planet from whence she came. Perhaps it's time we took a good, hard look at what it *really* takes to balance the many worlds of a working woman. Maybe, just maybe, it's possible to live fully and fulfilled, making a contribution within our home and beyond, without being reduced to a quivering mass in the process.

I know Linda and I are tired of trying to live up to the image. So is Jenny. And Robyn. And Melita, Christine, and Ann. . . .

And I'm sure—quite sure—that there's a better way.

And I thought I was the only woman who couldn't leap tall buildings with a single bound.

We know you've done it. Just go ahead and admit it. We've *all* done it.

We've all invited friends over for dinner, then spent so much effort reclaiming the house that we're too exhausted to hold a decent conversation when our company arrives. My husband encourages my family to entertain at least once a month because he says it's the only way to:

1. Get the house cleaned.
2. Get a meal that doesn't come from a can.

Yet it seems to me that we do ourselves and each other a great disservice when we knock ourselves out to present a perfect image to visiting friends.

Because even though we all play this deceptive role in our own homes, we actually believe the ruse when we see it performed at someone else's. We actually walk away believing that other women are pulling it off: They're succeeding at being the perfect employee, perfect mother, perfect home-maker, perfect wife, perfect lover, *ad nauseum*. Which is just about as rational as thinking we all spend our weekends leaping tall buildings and running faster than bullets and stopping freight trains.

The fact is, no one is making the grade.

The *ultimate* fact is, the grade is simply unattainable.

In the early 1970s, Betty Friedan identified the "problem that has no name," referring to the discontent of women who were unfulfilled in exclusive roles as wives and moms. Friedan's book *The Feminine Mystique*[2] helped launch the feminist movement that changed the work world and women's lives forever. Nearly three decades later, Friedan observed in an interview that a woman thinks there is something wrong with her if she can't be a perfect corporate executive *and* a perfect wife and mother. She added that innumerable woman are facing the agonies of this double burden.

Serious word, *agonies*. It means "extreme and prolonged mental or bodily pain."

All across America, women are trying to leap the Empire State Building and are being impaled on the pinnacle.

According to *Newsweek:* "The rigors of building careers, cultivating intimate relationships and caring for children have proved more difficult than anyone could have anticipated in the first heady days of feminism."[3] An advice columnist writing in *Woman's Day* observed: "I am having deep misgivings about some of the fallout from the women's movement. I see too many men and women suffering from a new rat race, which is, 'I am going to have it all'—an impossible goal and the source of much unrest."[4] Coauthor Linda has summed it up by saying, "If having it all means doing it all, can't I have just a little less?"

Okay. So Superwoman is nothing more than a comic book character, after all. And we're all catching on at about the same time.

Next question: What are we going to do about it?

I have a family. I have a job.
Do I have a problem?

Melita, thirty-seven, wears her raven-black hair shoulder length. She jokes about the dozen or so strands of gray at her temples, saying she'd buy one of those home color kits if she could find a spare three minutes to walk down that extra aisle at the supermarket. Sitting behind her desk at the bank, vibrant in a red wool suit, she looks like she just stepped from the pages of a fashion magazine. But when she talks about her life as a working mom, the image she paints is far from picture-perfect.

"Don't get me wrong," she says. "I've seen women who actually seem to be doing it—combining life at the office with life at home, and coming out okay. But these women are rare. Sometimes I wonder if it's an impossible undertaking—if you want any peace in your life, that is.

"But I don't wonder about it too long, for two reasons, I guess. First, I don't have a choice. I'm raising Brenda by myself ever since Frank left. And the second reason I can't think about it much is simply that I don't have that kind of luxury time. I'm racing all the time, always a single step ahead of crisis. It's not a great way to live, but maybe that's what being a working mom is all about. Maybe a job plus a family equals stress, and there's not much I can do about it. "

Does career plus family equal disaster? It sure seems that way at times, doesn't it? Time and time again—try as we might to find a more appropriate answer—we add two and two and end up, somehow, with Godzilla.

And if we don't end up with disaster, we get—at the very least—a nagging feeling that things could be better . . .

Or a bone-weariness, spiked by restless stress, that hangs on like a summer cold . . .

Or ravaging guilt, as tenacious as a pit bull, reminding us daily that we're not meeting the standard at home *or* at the office.

Yet Linda and I believe that career plus family doesn't *have* to equal disaster.

So what's the problem?

Maybe the problem is that too many women add a third element to the combination of family and career. Like the straw that broke the camel's back, we often add something else to the already precarious balance of family and job.

For many of us, the equation looks more like this:

Family + career + X = disaster.

Element "X" can be our link to crisis. After all, hydrogens and carbons create nothing more harmful than gasoline. But add nitrogen, and the result can kill you. Equal parts of hydrogen, carbon, and nitrogen become hydrogen cyanide, the stuff used in gas chambers.

Have you unknowingly mixed up a toxic combination in your life? If so, what's the "X" in *your* equation?

- It might be unrealistic expectations.
- It might be disorganization.
- It might be incompatibility between a particular job and home life.
- It might be some kind of self-destructive behavior stemming from a gaping void or wound in your life.

Many writers have addressed the issue of unrealistic expectations. Most of them tell us the way to cope is to simply lower our expectations. It's that easy.

To lower your expectations and find bliss as a working woman:

- Just settle for a less-than-sterile kitchen floor.
- Simply eat out more often and accept eating out of cans when you do eat at home.
- Don't bake six kinds of yuletide sweets. Pick up a couple Mrs. Smith's instead.

Other books don't suggest that we change our expectations. These books point to organization as the key.

- If our cupboards were better organized . . .
- If our children were trained to do more chores . . .
- If we remembered our daily devotions and took an hour each week to do something for "us" . . .
- If we cooked in larger batches, sorted the laundry as we undressed each day, and organized our wardrobe in three mix-and-match colors . . .
  then we could easily find the time to balance our varied worlds.

None of these suggestions are bad. In fact, as you read on you'll find a lot of practical ideas to help you lower your expectations and organize your time. You'll even find a chapter on dysfunctional behavior as well as on compatibility between your professional career and your career of being a mother and/or wife.

But maybe, to find success as a working woman, we've got to delve deeper. Perhaps it doesn't begin with how organized we are or how much dirt we can tolerate, although these things may come in handy later on.

Linda and I believe that success begins, instead, with matters of the heart and mind. Before we can talk about ways to improve what we *do*, we need to take a good look at who we *are*.

That's not easy to do. Especially when we live in a society that teaches men and women to pay more attention to their roles than to their souls.

Yet each of us is far more than the sum of our roles. Learning to see ourselves as whole persons, rather than seeing ourselves as the sum of our parts, is a foundation that can enable us to find success and even joy in the midst of a never-ending itinerary of things to do.

Notes

1. Elsa Houtz, *The Working Mother's Guide to Sanity* (Eugene, Oreg.: Harvest House Publishers, 1989), p. 15.

2. Betty Frieden, *The Feminine Mystique* (New York: Dell Publishing, 1984).

3. Eloise Salholz, Pamela Ambramson, Shawn Doherty, Renee Michael, and Diane Weathers, "Feminism's Identity Crisis," *Newsweek* (March 31, 1986), p. 58.

4. Eda LeShan, "Talking It Over," *Woman's Day* (January 17, 1989), p. 10.

2

Who Am I?

Healing the Rift Inside

Sometimes I think something got
lost in the shuffle: *Me.*

Christine is a spunky redhead with a full-time nursing career. She's not one to spout in a baby voice to her patients,
"Now this little shot won't hurt a bit." No, Christine's the kind
of nurse who says warmly but firmly, "Pull 'em down, touch
your toes, and grit your teeth so you don't scare the patients in
the next room when you scream." She's a realist. Which may be
why she's so frank about her life as a working mom.

"The hardest thing for me is keeping my two lives separate. I'm supposed to give 100 percent on the job, then walk
out the door and leave all my work problems and frustra-
tions in the parking lot. And I've got to do it, too, because
once I walk in the door at home I've got four people waiting
on me to give 100 percent all over again.

"Dan helps, you know," she says, tucking a carrot-colored
lock of hair behind one ear. "But I'm still the primary party
responsible for the kids and the meals and the house. This
goes on until seven in the morning, when I pull into the lot at
the hospital. And then suddenly I'm not even supposed to

remember that I've got kids and a family. My boss doesn't want to hear that my eight-year-old has the flu or that my baby, Paulie, clung to me like a barnacle when I tried to drop him off at my mom's."

My friend Robyn speaks of another kind of fragmentation. The mother of a preschooler and a first grader, Robyn reentered the work force last spring when husband, Jason, experienced a drop in sales. Now she's an administrative assistant at a company that makes copying machines.

"When I'm on the job," she explains, "I have to separate myself from all the features that make me a good wife and mom at home. Instead of being nurturing, I have to be aggressive. Instead of being patient, I have to demand results. Instead of being sensitive, I've got to be tough. It's hard to switch gears at the end of the day."

Dr. Harriet Braiker, in her book *The Type E Woman*, explains:

> Obviously, a certain degree of separateness . . . between the career woman persona and that of the wife, mother or girlfriend is appropriate. . . . But when the distinctions reach the point where you begin to feel like one person in a work setting and another person entirely in your personal relationships, something is amiss. . . .
>
> Changing hats so many times a day . . . is inherently stressful. But changing not only what you *do* but also who you *are*, including how you think of yourself, is an exhausting, confusing and overtaxing psychological costume change.[1]

Superman had it easy. He had two roles to manage. Only two. Part of the time he was cute but fumbling Clark Kent. The rest of the time he was a dashing and powerful superhero.

Today's men have it relatively easy, too. Their roles might include employee, husband, father, friend. Yet each of these roles relies on a similar set of personality traits. Wrong or right, our society expects men to be aggressive, dominant, independent, self-sufficient, analytical, and comfortable with leadership. These characteristics are seen as appropriate on the job *or* in the marriage. Despite their many roles, men can usually approach each of their roles as pretty much the same "self."

But for women, particularly working women, the challenge of becoming a different person for every role can be exhausting. The office demands a tiger, but the husband prefers a lamb. The kids need a hybrid of disciplinarian, playmate, and friend. The church wants a servant.

Before long, you feel like you're lost in a carnival house of mirrors. Every time you turn around, you see a new distortion or fraction of yourself, and not one of them reflects the real you. If you set up housekeeping long enough in a house of mirrors, the day finally arrives when you struggle to remember what the whole, original you actually looks like.

And you haven't got the slightest idea.

Three blind men described an elephant. One man, touching the trunk, described the elephant as a snake; the second man, at the tail, said the elephant was like a rope; the third man, near a leg, said the beast was like a tree.

Ann was bathing Brittney when the phone rang. She left the five-year-old playing with the sponge, crossed the hall into the bedroom, and picked up the receiver with wet hands.

"Hi, honey. Catch you at a bad time?" said a voice on the other end of the line.

"Hi, Mom. Nah, Brittney's finishing her bath, but I can hear her from here. What's up?"

"Not much. You've just been on my mind." Ann's mom inquired after Brittney, Ann's husband, Rick, and the new baby due in five months. Finally, she asked about Ann. "What about you, honey? How are you doing?"

"Me? Oh, fine. The morning sickness is gone, and I'm almost ready to give my presentation for the Sheffield Bank account—"

"I don't want to know about Ann the ad executive, or Ann the wife, or Ann the mother. How are *you*?"

The line fell silent. Finally Ann laughed. "After all that, Mom, I don't think there's anyone left."

But both women knew it wasn't a joke.

Sometimes we get so caught up in perfecting the right performance for each role that we lose sight of the whole person. Like the blind men describing an elephant, we tend to define ourselves in terms of our parts, rarely thinking of ourselves in any complete or integrated form. To make matters worse, there are unfortunately few situations in which responding as a "whole woman" is acceptable. Instead, we're often expected to respond to various circumstances with half our personality, keeping the other half under wraps.

■ If we want to succeed at the office, we often feel the need to act like a man, stifling our "feminine traits" until we're at home. One study asked men and women to select adjectives that best characterized *women*. They were then asked to identify words that described *men*. Finally, they were asked to select adjectives that best described a *successful leader* in the business world.

The lists for men and for leaders were nearly identical. None of the typically feminine traits were considered appropriate for leadership. Obviously, if a woman is going to be seen as promotion material in the corporate world, she's going to feel pressure to set aside stereotypical womanly qualities and replace them with perceived masculine traits.

■ Many men—regardless of how progressive they see themselves—prefer and even expect their women to fulfill a more traditional role at home. They may feel more comfortable with dependence and other supposedly feminine traits, while feeling vaguely threatened with the independence and assertiveness their wife or girlfriend is developing on the job.

■ Finally, even in the church, both men and women are subtly discouraged from revealing certain facets of themselves. One awkward area is that of our sexuality. Another is that of our imperfections. It's acceptable to admit that we're imperfect at the time of our salvation, but once we've attained any level of Christian maturity, our struggles are best kept to ourselves. In some churches, women who reveal any initiative beyond the realms of women's luncheons, Sunday school, or baking duty are going to draw wagging fingers and clucking tongues from fellow Christians.

After hanging up the phone and returning to Brittney's bath, Ann struggled with her mother's words, and with the vague uneasiness they created within her. As much as she hated the thought, Ann had to admit that she had no idea who she was outside of her roles. She used to know, or thought she knew, when she was in high school and college. Now she rarely thinks of herself as anyone other than Ann the professional, Ann the mom, or Ann the wife.

Ann helped Brittney climb from the tub, then scooped her up in a thick, warm towel. Later, when Brittney had been read to and prayed with and tucked snugly into bed, Ann turned out the lights and headed toward the living room to join Rick, who was watching television.

One last thought remained lodged in her head.

Last week, in a strategy meeting at the ad agency where Ann works, one of the women on Ann's creative team broke into tears, frustrated over the sudden cancellation of a project she'd spent the last three months setting up. As she struggled in vain to fight the tears, the woman apologized through clenched teeth. "I hate this," she said, then added, "As a woman, I guess I've just been raised to be emotional. But I'm working to get past all that."

At the time, Ann identified with her colleague's struggle to separate part of her "womanness" from her role at the office. She also empathized with her thwarted effort to portray the appropriate image. It was as if someone had stopped her in a crowded room and announced for everyone to hear, "Pardon me, but your womanhood is showing."

As Ann nestled into a corner of the couch beside Rick and caught the last five minutes of "Home Improvement," she was plagued by the uneasy thought that maybe separating herself into neat little categories wasn't such a good idea. What if something slipped through the cracks? What if, when it was all said and done, she lost something priceless? Was it possible to end up with *less* than she had at the beginning, when she began this quest to have it all?

Popsicles, pee pee, and a personal checking brochure.

Thursday afternoon, at 3:17, disaster struck.

A client returned my call.

"Karen? Scott Vandeventer here. Just got your message."

"Scott. Yes. Of course." As I stalled for time to sort out the confusion in my head, Kaitlyn stood just out of reach, struggling to tear the wrapper off a Popsicle that threatened to drip past her hands and into a puddle on the kitchen floor before she could accomplish her task.

"Is this a bad time?" asked the voice on the phone.

"Bad time? Well, um, of course not. I just wanted to ask you, oh, something about, uh . . . "

I raced to clear my head of Care Bears and Play-Doh and Popsicles shaped like Mickey Mouse.

"Oh yeah. I wanted to run an idea past you regarding the Personal Checking brochure I'm working on. . . ."

I began to breathe again. I had pulled it off. My secret was safe.

The executive V.P. of a successful credit union didn't have to know that I was actually human, with an entire other life that revolved around "Sesame Street" and macaroni and cheese.

He didn't have to know that he had thrown me into an emotional spin cycle by returning my call during my "Mommy" time and not during my "professional" time.

And maybe I could actually maintain the image of being 100 percent immersed in the role of professional writer without letting anyone—even myself—in on the secret that there's more to Karen Linamen than what I happen to "do" twenty or thirty hours every week.

Kaitlyn suddenly dropped the unopened Popsicle on the kitchen floor and ran to the window to watch a bluejay poised in the pine tree outside. As sticky red syrup oozed from the wrapper onto the floor, my concentration oozed away as well. While trying to explain my concepts for the content and graphics of a marketing device, I found myself on hands and knees, craning my neck to keep my ear pinned to the receiver, while stretching to reach the gooey wrapper on my kitchen floor. It was just out of reach.

I stood up, turned my back on the Popsicle, and tried to refocus my attention on the phone conversation. I almost did it, too, when suddenly a small hand tugged at my leg.

"Mama, I have to go potty."

"Uh, Scott? Could you hold the line just a moment?"

I put the phone down and dropped to the floor to unhook Kaitlyn's overalls. "Don't forget to wipe," I whispered as she turned to hobble toward the bathroom, her pants around her ankles.

I reclaimed the receiver and regeared my thoughts, but the transition I was counting on didn't come in time. I opened my mouth and blurted, "Okay, I'm back. My daughter just needed to go pee pee."

I froze.

Scott just laughed. Not the laugh of an executive vice-president, but the laugh of a dad, big and warm and real. We finished the conversation and began negotiating a time for me to stop by the office and drop off the first draft of some copy. I tried one last time to recoup my image, suggesting times when I could drop by, all the while mentally figuring which morning I'd be most likely to find an available sitter. But Scott already knew my secret. I'm not Superwriter. I'm human. And I'm a human with a family.

"Look," he said, "on trips like this when you just need to drop something off, feel free to bring your daughter. In fact, if the need arises, you can bring her along even if we've got a meeting scheduled. We could work in the board room, where she could read or play, and you and I could cover whatever we needed to. I know what it's like," he added. "We've got two little girls. So I try to be flexible."

Scott understood that I was more than a writer. He knew my secret, and he could live with it. Could I?

It would be nice to feel like a "whole" person.
But I'm not greedy. On a lot of days
I'd settle for just feeling human.

When I learned that a client could accept me as a whole person, I felt free. I felt respected for who I *am* as well as for what I *do*. I also felt relieved.

But not every story has a happy ending.

One woman I know recently launched a successful home business selling decorative gift baskets. Her husband, however, can't accept her business acumen and refuses to recognize her efforts beyond that of a hobby. Despite the fact that he has an MBA and could provide valuable insights as his wife charts entrepreneurial waters for the first time, this man is finding it difficult to respond to all aspects of his wife's personhood.

Christine, who we met earlier, has one complaint about her work at the hospital: "That head nurse is a maniac. If any one of us dares ask for special scheduling for personal matters, she fumes and frowns and sputters. It's like she rejects the idea that anyone should have any life beyond their profession. It's a big problem."

On the other extreme, Robyn's manager at the copier company can't seem to get past the idea that Robyn is a woman. Too often her assignments revolve around refilling the coffee machine and supervising kitchen duty rather than administrating the kind of responsible projects assigned to her male counterparts.

But women aren't the only people asked to fill a role at the expense of the whole person. For generations, men have been squeezed into a stereotype that didn't have room for "wimpy" characteristics like sensitivity, fear, doubt, compassion.

Generations of little boys have been taught to avoid emotions like the plague, to punch back instead of cry when their turn came to meet the school bully. Our men have been trained to sacrifice personal wholeness and family life at the altar of corporate achievement. They've been raised to believe the myth that they *are* what they do at the office—no more, no less.

Somewhere in the 1970s, the "Tough Guy Ideal" went belly-up. The Macho Man, once every woman's dream, suddenly became the butt of jokes. Archie Bunker became a sort of national "unhero." Now macho is out and *thirtysomething* is in. Yet men who *are* ready to explore personal frontiers often find their efforts thwarted. When Christine's third child was born, Dan asked his boss for an extended leave so he could spend several weeks at home while his family adjusted to its newest member. The request was denied.

Men are *just now* being encouraged to live integrated lives. There are still a lot of roadblocks in their way, but the fact remains that men still have fewer roles for which they need to perfect their performances. Without lessening the tragedy of the crime, society has fairly consistently demanded the same things of American men. Even as women have gone back to work in droves, restructuring home life as well as the working world, the role of our men has changed comparatively little.

The husband of a stay-at-home mom spends a daily average of 40 minutes in child care and housework. The man whose wife works outside the home spends a daily average of 20 additional minutes in child care and housework, despite the fact that his wife has just increased her daily work load by eight to ten hours. Although research tells us that the trend is starting to change—and that men are starting to become more involved on the home front—the primary role for most men continues to be that of breadwinner.

But a working woman is hard-pressed to name her primary role. Is it co-breadwinner? After all, that's where she spends the majority of her hours. Or is her primary role that of mother, since she usually remains the primary caretaker of her children? Her primary role could easily be that of home-maker, since the majority of household chores remain her responsibility. Or is she, first and foremost, a wife?

The fact is, even as we make the effort to integrate our lives, we hit pockets of resistance. Sometimes the resistance comes from those around us. Sometimes it comes from within ourselves.

But just pretend with me a moment. Pretend you just won a state-of-the-art home entertainment system on "Wheel of Fortune." Pretend you just won a million dollars in the Publisher's Clearinghouse Sweepstakes. Now imagine something that could very well change your life more dramatically than technology or buying power. Imagine you could see yourself as a whole person in every arena of your life. Imagine you weren't a victim—as well as a perpetrator—of the stifling stereotypes that accompany each of your many roles. What differences might that mean in your life?

- **Less stress,** for one thing. Change, even of a positive sort, creates stress. Every time we shift between our many "persons," we're experiencing stress of major proportions. Working women will always face the transitions between our roles as employee and mother and wife and daughter and friend, etc. But we can face these transitions more effectively if we can do so as relatively the same person.

- **Occasional snickers ... or worse.** Let's face it. A boss might not appreciate that we aren't as available for overtime because kids and/or husbands deserve a place in our schedules as well. We might even lose out on a promotion or a prestigious new responsibility.

There may also be adjustments on the home front, as husbands or kids are introduced to a side of ourselves that we've managed to hide up till now. Women friends, who are still struggling to present the appropriate stereotype in the appropriate settings, may scold and nag and shake their heads over our newfound freedom. But don't get discouraged. Read on.

■ **Greater self-confidence** as we eventually develop a well-balanced self that "works" in every situation. We'll never be truly confident if we remain "on guard" lest a client be reminded of our motherhood; lest colleagues see us cry and be reminded of the fact that we're women; or lest the men in our lives catch us making a competent decision and have to face the fact that there's more to us than an apron and/or negligee.

■ A little bit of **inner peace** despite the hurricane that carries us through our days. For a working woman, the daily calendar fills up quickly with projects or meetings or clients or patients. There are also dentists and supermarkets and Little League and laundry, car-pools and preschools and the annual Christmas party for hubby's office. The car breaks down, the washing machine floods the kitchen, and a teenage daughter comes home from a date with her first broken heart. With all that in your life, who needs a storm on the inside, too?

■ **The best possible role model** for the next generation of working women, and the men who'll live and work with them!

Last Sunday our pastor told a story from the pulpit about a woman whose husband died suddenly from a heart attack. The couple's six-year-old daughter struggled greatly to adjust to her father's death. Meanwhile, mom worked hard to reestablish a life for herself and her daughter.

Eight months after the death, the mother was tucking her daughter into bed when the child announced: "I wish you had loved Daddy."

"Honey, how can you say that?" the woman gasped. "I loved your daddy very much. I still love him. I always will."

The little girl remained firm. "Then how come I never saw you cry?"

"Believe me, I cried. I cried myself to sleep every night for months after Daddy died."

The little girl fell silent. A moment later she said simply, "I wish you would have cried with me."

There's something to be said for maintaining an image. But if our children are going to develop healthy perspectives on life, one of the greatest gifts we can give them is the privilege of seeing Mom in her entirety. Linda and I wish we could give you a list of dos and don'ts that would enable you to suddenly start seeing yourself as an integrated whole—but it's not that simple. It's a process, a journey, a discovery that each of us makes on her own. The following chapters will continue to examine the importance of this journey. Hopefully, they will help you as you embark on your own—because an integrated life is, and forever will be, far greater than the sum of its roles.

Notes

1. Harriet Braiker, *The Type E Woman* (New York: Nal Penguin, Inc., 1986), p. 92.

3

Setting Boundaries

*Great Expectations:
One of the Things You Don't
Want to Add to the Mix of
Job and Family*

"But, Mom, *everybody else* is doing it!"

Do you remember those conversations with your folks? The ones during which you counted off all the really neat things your friends got to *do* that you didn't? You might have mentioned staying up till midnight, watching R movies, or going on the overnight field trip at school. Or maybe the conversation took a slight twist, as you described all the great things your peers *had* that you didn't have: a C-cup figure, a cuter boyfriend, a brand-new car, straighter teeth, or curly hair . . . .

At that point, your parents probably countered with a list of privileges, talents, or circumstances that were unique to you. But it didn't make any difference, did it? You still expected to be just like everyone else. And when those expectations—as unrealistic as they were—didn't come true, it hurt.

Linda and I have just one question: Why are we still at it?

■ I feel a pang in my self-esteem every time I visit Jenny's apartment and find her kitchen counter clear of dirty dishes. At my house, Larry and I haven't seen our kitchen counter for a long time. I think it's yellow. At least, it was yellow last Christmas when I caught my last glimpse of it. And while I'm lamenting my failure at the "white glove" test, I overlook the fact that I manage to write books, spend the majority of every day with my daughter, and serve my family about three balanced meals each week.

■ Jenny knows I covet the tidy, inviting atmosphere she maintains in her home, but she can't quite forgive herself for the fact that she's handier with a can opener than with a measuring cup. Last week, she cooked two meals from scratch. It took a lot of effort, but the meals were actually on the table by 7:00 P.M. By the second night, she was feeling pretty great about her accomplishments, when Jeff made a really unfortunate comment: "Dinner was great and all, honey, but I don't need a lot of gourmet stuff. Could we just eat at a more reasonable time? Like five?"

Jeff's still trying to get the chicken divan stains out of his best shirt.

■ Ann, on the other hand, serves balanced meals, keeps her kitchen clean, and never goes to bed without taking off all her makeup. But she grinds her teeth over the fact that she never has enough time or energy to invest on her job. Advertising is a competitive industry; Ann feels hindered by the fact that she can't work the overtime hours that her male colleagues do, and that morning sickness kept her home a couple mornings each week for nearly a month.

We couldn't have it all as kids; we can't have it all today. Yet many of us have expectations that are just as unrealistic as the ones we had as adolescents.

Our fairytale expectations come in two forms. First, we may have *unrealistic standards*: We want to "have it all." Like the thirteen-year-old who grieves because she doesn't look like Cindy Crawford, we often establish a standard of performance that may not be appropriate for who we are at our current stage in life. I didn't look like a movie star or model at thirteen—nor at thirty, darn it! And there are other standards of performance, at home and on the job, that are equally unreasonable. For example, I think the standard of a spotless house had better wait till my kids are grown and/or I retire from the work force. A standard of pursuing my career as if it were the only priority in my life is also unrealistic at this stage in my life.

Second, unrealistic expectations exist in a *life that has no boundaries*. Would we let a seventeen-year-old "do it all"? Stay up till dawn? Join the band, basketball team, pep squad, and computer club? Hold down a full-time job while taking college-level courses? If we did, we would doom her to failure. Yet we set ourselves up for the same crash landing when we insist we can handle every project or responsibility related to career, family, church, and social life.

There are twenty-four hours in each day. No more, no less. Every woman—and every man—needs to do some serious soul searching and decide how she or he wants to spend those hours.

Nobody can have it all. *Nobody* can do it all.

Not women. Not men.

And most important, not all at the same time.

Nobody can have it all—
but everybody gets to choose.

I approached the office door with sweaty palms. The words "Agency of Sanity Management" were stenciled on the glass pane. Reminding myself that Linda Holland had recommended this place highly, I took a deep breath and opened the door.

I signed my name on the check-in sheet, picked up a back issue of *Life*, and took a seat on the squeaky leatherette couch. A moment later a receptionist called my name and motioned me toward the door to the inner sanctum. A counselor met me there and ushered me into a small but comfortable office.

"Let's see. You are . . . " The woman looked down at my application. "Karen. Well, Karen, welcome to Sanity Management. I'm Mrs. Morrison. I see on your form that Linda Holland recommended you."

I nodded.

"Very sharp woman, Linda. And a regular client. Did she tell you much about our agency?"

I shook my head.

"Well, basically, there are four plans—priority management strategies, really—to choose from," Mrs. Morrison explained. "We believe that by recognizing and selecting a plan up front, a man or woman can achieve a much greater level of effectiveness and satisfaction over the period of a lifetime. Of course, there are many opportunities during a life period in which someone, like yourself, can exchange one plan for another. But first you've got to make a choice. Are you ready?"

"I don't know . . ."

"Fine." Mrs. Morrison pulled a three-ring notebook from a drawer and turned to the first page, which featured the photograph of a sitcom actress familiar from 1960s television or from the Nickelodeon channel on cable. "Your first option is the 'Harriet Nelson Plan.' This means you get to do all the fun homemaking things that sound really great at seven-fifteen as you're rushing out the door with kids, sack lunches, file folders, and the half-off pizza coupon you're going to use that night for dinner.

"As Harriet Nelson, you get to greet the kids at the front door on rainy afternoons and enjoy relaxed, private moments—not often enough—but more often than you could if you added an outside job to your schedule. You get to build friendships with the growing number of women who have made the same choice to stay home. You might even get to make an investment in an interest, cause, or ministry that you wouldn't have time for if you were working full-time."

I studied the notebook. "That doesn't sound bad."

"If you're interested in this option, I've got a stack of references I can give you."

"Great!"

Mrs. Morrison flipped the page. "Your second option is the 'Lee Iacocca Plan.' Enjoy the respect and friendship of colleagues, climb the corporate ladder, play the overtime game, feel pride in your accomplishments, develop your professional potential. Give 100 percent, and enjoy the advancement, prestige and material comfort that will accompany your efforts. There's not much time left for home life, relationships, that sort of thing. But it's still satisfying in its own way. I've got a stack of references on this one, too—mostly from men. They've been selecting this option for centuries."

"I like that one, too."

The counselor nodded. "Well, you're welcome to it. In the past thirty years or so, a lot more women have gone this route, either long-term or for shorter periods of time than the men."

"Short-term? How does that work?" I asked.

"The short-term approach brings us to option three, which is the 'Ping-Pong Plan,'" Mrs. Morrison explained.

"Ping-Pong?"

"Sure, because you bounce back and forth. Between college and kids, you get to make your mark on the corporate world. Then, as soon as the diapers appear, you're on maternity sabbatical. Play kickball, make paper dolls, relieve your husband of a few of the house chores he handled while you brought home half the bacon. You may choose to take a few classes or work a few hours a week to maintain your professional skills, but for the most part you'll be able to raise your kids without the distractions that come with working full-time outside the home.

"A few years down the road, when your children are in elementary school, junior high or high school, you can pick up your profession again," Mrs. Morrison added. "You will have lost momentum and dollars, and you may never catch up with colleagues who skipped the maternity sabbatical. But you'll have memories and achievements that they'll never have.

"I can give you references for this one, too. A surprising number of influential women have gone with this option and have been very pleased with the results—Sandra Day O'Connor, Jean Kirkpatrick, Geraldine Ferraro, among others."

"No kidding!"

"Finally," she said, "option number four is our popular 'Custom Plan.' If you are currently juggling a family and a full- or part-time job, this is your plan. Please note that it has nothing whatsoever to do with Harriet Nelson or Lee Iacocca. It's a personalized plan that you and your family have to create for yourselves, and it may contain some of the components of the Harriet Nelson or Lee Iacocca Plan. Then again, it may not."

"What's *that* supposed to mean?" I asked.

"Pardon me?"

"What do you mean it might not contain *all* the components of Plans One or Two? That's what I want!"

"No, no, you don't understand. If you want *all* the components of Harriet Nelson, you need to select Plan One. If you want *all* the components of Lee Iacocca, then you need to select Plan Two. Plan One and Plan Two are exclusive packages. That means while you are 100 percent engrossed in either plan, you automatically waive your claim to the other."

"But I've got to have both!" I exclaimed, grabbing the notebook and clutching it to my chest.

"Look, don't get hostile with me!" Mrs. Morrison huffed. "I don't make the rules. Each plan comes with its own set of benefits, disadvantages, priorities, expectations. . . . You've got to choose."

"I don't think I can," I said sadly.

The counselor sighed, long and heavy. "If you can't—*really can't*—choose between the plans, well, there's one other alternative."

My heart leaped. "Tell me!"

"I'm not really supposed to. I mean, it's not agency-approved. In fact, it's sort of experimental, and we have reason to believe it's not even, well, healthy."

"Just tell me. I think that's the one I want."

"Okay." She shrugged. "It's option number five, where you get to combine the complete roles of Harriet Nelson and Lee Iacocca. It's called the 'Nervous Breakdown Plan.' "

"I don't care what it's called. Just let me see the references, then tell me how to sign up."

"References? Well, um, you see, that's why it's not agency-approved. There are lots of women selecting this plan. But no one, it seems, is willing to recommend it."

"The more we run around trying to do everything, the less able we are to do that which God has given us to do."[1]

Ann admits that she opted for Plan Five, and has been chin-deep in unrealistic standards since day one:

- ■ She holds herself to impossible standards in her home, trying to keep house and family like her mother did, even though her mom never worked outside the home.

- ■ She also holds herself to impossible standards in her job, trying to compete with men who can give more time and energy to their career than she can because they've got wives at home picking up the slack.

As a result, Ann nearly buckles under the guilt when she can't live up to the standards.

Robyn is another victim of Plan Five, but she struggles with unrealistic expectations regarding her boundaries. She just can't say no!

- ■ In addition to her full-time job and her responsibilities at home, Robyn just registered four-year-old Rachel for a tumbling class that requires parent participation.

- ■ When a friend at church had her new baby, Robyn volunteered to coordinate a week's worth of meals for the new mother.

■ Last week, Jason asked Robyn to prepare sandwiches and dessert for a motivational seminar he's organizing at the office. Robyn agreed without a second thought.

■ When Robyn's boss asked for a volunteer to handle a problem with an important client, Robyn felt the need to prove herself to her boss as well as to her coworkers. She took on the project, even though it meant several evenings away from home.

Fairytale expectations regarding standards and/or boundaries can come from any combination of the following sources:

- The way successful women and men are portrayed in the media
- The unflawed image of ourselves that we like to present to each other
- The way Mom did things (we forget we've got an outside job she didn't have)
- The way colleagues without families (or with wives who handle the majority of responsibilities at home) do things
- The way we used to do things before we combined making a home with making a living

Any way we look at it, unrealistic expectations are hard to shake. While many of us may claim to have abandoned them for a more realistic approach, we agonize each time we fall short of an expectation we supposedly dumped.

So how do we adjust unrealistic expectations? Can we indeed cancel our subscription to the unattainable demands we impose on ourselves? How do we go about developing a more personalized and workable approach to our lives?

Limits are wicked. Boundaries are poison.
Fences and walls are dastardly evils.
And if you believe that, I've got this real estate
in Florida I'd like to talk to you about. . . .

For the majority of my childhood, my mom didn't work outside the home. That meant someone was there to greet me when I walked in the front door brimming with stories and feelings from my day at school. It meant home-baked cookies, trips to the library, and picnics at the park, where Mama read *Tom Sawyer* aloud beneath cottony summer clouds. I watched this woman raise three girls, run a house, and love a man, serving him cheerfully when he dragged home in the evenings and giggling like a schoolgirl in love when he called home from work in the middle of the day just to say hi. I didn't miss a thing. I watched and internalized all the steps and secrets to succeeding and thriving in a traditional role at home. I wanted to be just like her.

But there were also the evenings I fell asleep in my dad's lap, listening with him to reel-to-reels that outlined the steps to possibility thinking. There were late-night talks that went way past my bedtime, as my dad shared his thoughts about God and the tremendous potential he places in the hearts, souls, and minds of men and women. I remember spouting goose flesh as I pondered the unlimited opportunities that awaited me as soon as I got out of elementary school. I was pretty sure, even then, that I wanted to be a writer. But who could know for sure? I could, after all, do anything of which I dared to dream.

About that time, I began to take note of that first heady decade of the women's movement. I still remember seeing smoldering piles of blackened Playtex on the six o'clock news. Suddenly I knew, without a doubt, that I could embrace my mom's world and my dad's world with a single, boundless stretch. The limits of my sex were being stripped away even as I matured. I could do everything!

As a young woman, I looked into my future and saw *freedom from* boundaries. I would never have to choose between being traditional or liberated. I could do it all. But instead of assuming I'd be free from all limits, I should have realized that I was being given the *freedom to* define my own world, to set my own limits.

Freedom from boundaries equals disaster.

Freedom to establish our own boundaries equals opportunity.

There's nothing wrong with limits. In fact, they can actually protect and provide a framework for growth.

Dr. James Dobson, in his film series *Turn Your Heart toward Home*, explains that a child in an unfenced playground will often feel overwhelmed by the openness. Instead of exploring and playing, the child will hover, insecure, in the center of the yard. In a secure, fenced setting, however, that same child will confidently explore the territory, marching right up to the boundaries and becoming comfortable with them. In time, as feelings of self-confidence and security increase, the boundaries may be extended.

Boundaries are necessary. They're healthy. They're even desirable.

One evening a friend, Keith Wall, and I were driving home following an emotionally draining interview for a book we were writing on AIDS. We had just picked up Kaitlyn from my parents' home, where she'd spent the evening, and were on our way to drop Keith off at his car. On the way, crisis struck. Kaitlyn—who was at that time two years old—got bored in her car seat.

Have you ever tried to drive (and survive) while a two-year-old unleashes her fury in the back seat? Trying to cap a hurricane in a pop bottle would be easier. I threatened. I bribed. I cajoled. I promised spankings, soap in the mouth, and, looking ahead, a month's restriction immediately following her sixteenth birthday. But Kaitlyn continued to scream and groan and kick and wrestle with her seat belt until I pulled into the parking lot where Keith's Mazda waited.

By now Kaitlyn had managed to wiggle out of the car seat, and while Keith and I wrapped up our business, I let her play with the stuffing from a hole in the upholstery (moms learn to accept peace and quiet on almost any terms). Eventually Keith climbed out of my car and into his own, and I ordered Kaitlyn back into her car seat.

She went, grudgingly. I started the engine. I was halfway through the parking lot when Kaitlyn announced, "You said you were going to spank me."

The memory came back fuzzily, diffused in my mind by the brain-scrambling decibel level that had been emanating from the back seat at the time.

"You're right. But Mama's too tired right now." I sighed. And then, knowing that consistency in discipline is important, I launched straight into a white lie. "But I'm going to spank you just like I promised. Tomorrow."

Kaitlyn was silent a moment. When she finally spoke, there was a bewildered edge to her voice. There was even a hint of hurt. In fact, in the rear-view mirror, I could see her lip curl into a pout and quiver as she said solemnly, "But you *tol'* me you were going to spank me."

Feeling utterly shamed, I pulled to the side of the road, crawled halfway into the back seat, took Kaitlyn from her car seat, and gave her the promised spanking. Afterward, as I held her in my arms, I peered into her eyes and asked, "Is that better now?"

She smiled. She nodded. And she gave me a hug.

Some boundaries are designed to rein in destructive behavior. If these kinds of boundaries are neglected in kids, even doting grandparents are hard-pressed to love the sad little tyrants that are the result. If adults ignore similar boundaries of law and ethics, the result may be the destruction of marriages, property, and/or lives.

There are other boundaries as well, boundaries such as limits on our time and limits to our energy. If we ignore these, we're setting ourselves up for heartburn at the very best—at the very worse, a straitjacket.

The next time you butt up against a boundary, don't resent it. Respect it. Honestly. If a two-year-old can grasp the value of a boundary, why can't we?

Notes

1. Interview with Judy Stewart, M.A., community relations and volunteer coordinator with the Women's Transitional Living Center, Inc., Orange, California.

Dishes? Nah, she sprays with Raid once a week
and calls it even.

4

Organization

*They Say a Messy Desk
Is the Sign of a Creative Mind.
It Could Also Signal Disaster If You're
Already Balancing Career and Family.*

What does the Pink Panther say
when he steps on an ant?
"Deadant, Deadant,
Deadant, Deadant, Deadant."[1]

It had been one of those weeks. I'd been up two nights in a row trying to meet a writing deadline. Larry had been burning the midnight oil as well, preparing for a speaking engagement and computer presentation coming up the following week.

By Thursday night, it was all we could do to eat dinner, get Kaitlyn to bed and stare, bleary-eyed, at the ten o'clock news. I kept hoping Larry would get up and log onto the computer so I would have an excuse to go to bed instead of working. Larry was waiting for me to start writing so he could proceed, guiltless, to bed. By 10:45 we gave up and decided we both deserved a good night's rest.

We helped each other off the couch and stumbled through the kitchen to the bedroom. My eyes were half closed, but I knew we were passing through the kitchen because of the smell of two days' worth of dishes, which had been overlooked in the deadline hustle.

I groaned. "I can't leave the dishes like this."

"Forget it," said Larry, pulling me along. "We'll do 'em together tomorrow. You need your sleep."

"You don't understand," I said, trying to shake myself awake. "There'll be a million ants in here tomorrow if I don't do something."

"Suit yourself." Larry shrugged and plodded toward the bathroom to brush his teeth. Five minutes later the bathroom door opened and he stumbled toward the bed, then stopped short and stared down where I lay curled beneath the covers. "That was fast work!" he said, a look of admiration in his eyes. Suddenly he turned his face, furrowed his brow and wrinkled his nose. "What's that smell?"

He wandered out the bedroom door and toward the kitchen.

I burrowed deeper beneath the blanket.

When he came back, the admiration in his eyes had been replaced by something else. I'm not exactly sure how to describe it.

"Karen, you didn't wash the dishes."

I wasn't sure if he was asking me or telling me. I pulled the covers higher and muttered, "I know."

"And there's Raid everywhere."

"I know. I sprayed all the dishes and the counter, too."

There was this long pause. Then he laughed. "Well, you did something, all right. We won't have to worry about the ants." He crawled into bed and turned out the light.

You know who you are.

If you're an organized person, please save me further humiliation by skipping on to the next chapter. If you're not an organized person, I know you won't hold anything in this chapter against me because you've probably done as bad or worse.

Jenny tells me she likes to come to my house because it reminds her that she's not the only person who falls short of Superwoman status. It's sort of a compliment. I think.

Anyway, I'm not going to enumerate all the benefits of organization and the hazards of slovenliness. If you're already organized, you've caught on. If you're not organized, you're painfully aware of the pitfalls of our way of life. Besides, there are countless excellent books on organization. Linda and I have even put together our own collection of helpful suggestions on this subject—and other topics of interest to working women—which is included in the handbook offered at the back of this book.

But allow me this single observation:

Mess enhances stress.

There is something to be said for having realistic expectations about the state of cleanliness in your home. But when the state of your home begins to have an adverse effect on your peace of mind (or when you run the risk of dying in your sleep due to excessive use of pesticides in the home), things have gone too far.

I don't care how you do it:

- Hire a cleaning service.
- Create a card file that tells you what day of the week to tackle each household chore.
- Enlist the help of husband, kids, neighbors and/or door-to-door salespeople.
- Move to a smaller house.
- Create a job board for your family.
- Set the oven timer for one hour and limit your household work to that one hour—you'll tend

to work quicker and smarter when your time is limited.

There are countless ways to do it. So just do it. Find a way to de-clutter your home, and you'll find less clutter in your head and heart as well.

I have one more thought on this subject (which Larry finds amazing—he says he never knew I had *any* thoughts regarding organization). While there are hundreds of suggestions and systems that will help you organize your life, there are no magic formulas.

Reasonably mess-less living is a day-to-day decision. Whatever method you choose to order your life (short of hiring a maid) will demand daily persistence on the part of you and your family. However, there will be times when the entire house falls into shambles within a twenty-four-hour period. When that happens, remember the chapter on expectations and laugh your way through it.

With that kind of balance—daily effort contrasted by reasonable expectations—you'll have the tools you need to create a less-than-perfect-but-better-than-chaos atmosphere in your home. After all, being a working woman comes with plenty of its own baggage and stresses. Coming home to a national disaster area is more than any of us should have to live with on a regular basis. Our home is the single place we can recoup and prepare for the next day's challenges. We owe it to ourselves and to our family to provide the kind of atmosphere that's worth coming home to.

Notes
1. Compliments of Stephen Shakarian, Karen's fourteen-year-old cousin.

5

Compatibility between Home and Career

Incompatibility Dissolves More than Marriages.
It Can Dissolve Your Sanity If
Your Job Is Incompatible with Your Other Roles.

You can't miss the signs.

Linda pulled into the parking lot a little after 2:00 A.M. and began maneuvering to find a somewhat lighted spot. She found one near the laundry room, locked the car behind her, and hurried toward her apartment at the far end of the complex. After waking Mrs. Hammond from where she slumped, nodding, in the easy chair, Linda made sure her elderly neighbor got back safely to her apartment next door, then undressed quietly so as not to wake her eight-year-old daughter, Tami, or two-year-old Christopher sleeping soundly in the back bedroom. Then she set the alarm for 7:30 A.M. and crawled into bed. It wasn't the most convenient job, taking the swing shift at the front desk at a major hotel chain, but it put food on the table in a city where jobs were hard to find. Best yet, it allowed Linda to take classes during the day.

Before drifting off to sleep, Linda thought of two-year-old Chris and ran a mental list of danger zones in the house. After she got Tami off to school at 8:00, Linda usually tried to catnap on the couch in the living room. Although she tried to maintain some awareness of Chris while she dozed, her son tended to find his own entertainment—not all of it desirable.

There had been the morning she awoke to the sound of rushing water. Stumbling from the couch and sloshing across a water-logged living-room carpet, she found Chris perched on the bathroom sink, waving a toilet plunger and assuring his mother, "I fix it, Mommy! I fix it!" He had plugged the drain with a washcloth and cranked both faucets fully open.

Another day, Chris decided to fix his own breakfast, making a neat pile of Kellogg's Cornflakes on the living-room carpet. Then he added the milk.

Yet another morning, Linda awoke to silence and knew, instinctively, there was trouble. She found the apartment empty and the front door ajar. Heart racing wildly, she flew down the steps and across the parking lot. Near the street she found a sock. On a neighbor's lawn she found the top to Chris's pajamas. A half-block away a second sock lay discarded near the curb. Just as she stooped to collect Chris's pajama bottoms from a flower garden, Linda spotted her son, frolicking naked down the sidewalk.

Lying in bed at 2:45 A.M., Linda reviewed all these disasters in her mind, then completed her mental check of the apartment. Front door bolted. Bathroom door locked. Breakfast cereal and milk beyond Christopher's reach. Somewhat confident that the apartment and her son were secure, she closed her eyes and let sleep come.

Roughly six hours later, at 9:00 A.M.—after Tami had left for school and Linda had gone back to sleep on the couch—something woke her up. Something on her face. Something soft and damp and faintly warm. She started, then pried her lids open and managed to focus her eyes on her son, stand-ing next to her. He was patting her cheek.

"Hi, hon," Linda mumbled. "Hey, do I smell . . . "

Suddenly Linda grabbed Chris by the wrist and yanked his hand from her face. She found herself staring at sticky brown fingers.

Chris smiled and wiggled his hand. "Mommy, Cristafer went poo poo!"

They say comedy is merely tragedy plus time. Now, sev-enteen years later, Linda can laugh about the incident. (Nine-teen-year-old Chris, however, may need more time. He didn't laugh at all when he found this story in the book.) But that single event did more than provide a future laugh for Linda. At the time, it helped her come to an important decision for herself and her family.

"The signs were everywhere I looked," she says today. "My kids, my house, my own body and emotions were all telling me that the schedule of that particular job wasn't working. Sure, the money was good, benefits decent, and the stress low. But the hours weren't a good match for *my* family at *that* time. So I got out."

Left untreated, incompatibility is terminal. It means you're *going* to fail at something: The job, your kids—maybe even your marriage.

Seven years ago, I was an editor with a well-known Chris-tian ministry. Although I had been writing part-time and free-lancing for years, this position marked my first full-time position in the field. And what a position!

It was fast paced. Challenging. Stimulating. Intoxicating! Surrounded by writers and editors and artists, I knew I'd found professional heaven! Working alongside the talents of a particular editor—the director of our department—I learned more about the craft of writing than I had in four years of college.

Unfortunately, the ministry was located forty miles north of my house, and the many evenings I chose to work late meant even later hours getting home. Other evenings, the staff would collectively catch a movie or grab a hamburger. We were too far away for Larry to join us, so I always went alone.

Soon Larry and I were developing friendships in completely different circles. Then we started attending a church that was forty minutes south of our home. Before long, we had friends not only in different circles, but scattered throughout three different counties! There was very little social time together. Private time together was pretty rare, as well.

In essence, we were drifting.

About that time, I was offered a position at the university where my husband taught, ten minutes from our house. It was a lateral move—same kind of position, same salary, similar responsibilities—but with a smaller staff, less prestige, less glamour. Still, I'd be close to home and close to Larry. Maybe we could even start sharing the same world again.

I won't kid you by saying it was an easy decision, because it wasn't. I felt a great loss at the prospect of leaving. I grieved inside, and I resented having to make that kind of choice. Finally, however, I gave my notice, boxed up my coffee mug and photographs, and moved forty miles south to a little office in La Mirada, California. I've never regretted the decision.

Nobody said life is fair.

The party was in full swing by the time Ann walked into the suite. A young man from Ann's creative team careened across the room toward her, balancing his sixth drink of the evening.

"Swell pardy," he breathed into her face.

Ann wrinkled her nose. "Remember the flight tomorrow, Mitch. You're gonna be sorry if you're not careful."

"I'll be jes fine. You wash and see. A'yway, I'm nodda one pre'nant. You are. If anyone's gonna get sick, i'll be you."

Ann, five months pregnant, just smiled. Mitch, spying a waiter with a fresh tray of drinks, teetered away. A moment later he was exchanging off-color jokes with Sheffield Bank's chairman of the board.

Ann settled into a chair with a cup of decaf coffee and watched the celebration. Sheffield Bank was one of their bigger accounts, and the ad campaign her team had helped put together was turning into a real coup for their agency.

She should have been feeling victory. Instead, there was a gnawing sensation in the pit of her stomach. And it wasn't the baby. It was the stress. The competition. The travel, pace, and energy demanded by her job, coupled with the constant pull she felt toward her responsibilities at home. Now, with a second baby on the way . . .

Ann took another sip of coffee. It tasted bitter, but not as bitter as she felt watching colleagues as they drank and laughed and partied. Some, like Mitch, were single. Others were married, yet none of them seemed distracted by families waiting for them at home. None of them seemed faced with the kinds of choices Ann had been brooding over the past few weeks.

It wasn't fair. It just wasn't fair.

Fact #1: Some jobs don't mix with a healthy home life.
Fact #2: No one's willing to admit it.

There are a lot of jobs that mix with home life about as well as oil and water—careers that require a lot of travel, a lot of overtime, or frequent transfers from city to city. The weird hours of other jobs mean that husbands and wives rarely cross paths, or that kids only see Dad on weekends. Sometimes the job is fine—but it's the unbalanced aggression of the person *in* that job that results in incompatibility with the home front.

How do some people choose to respond to incompatibility between career and family?

■ For generations, men in particular have pursued careers without considering the impact on their families. They've been able to get away with it because they've had wives at home, picking up the pieces that got dropped—pieces like raising the kids and managing the family. As a result, wives and kids have had to survive in the face of Dad's overtime, weekend hours, and sudden transfers to new locations.

■ In a related version of the story, men and women who are single and childless have been able to succeed in careers incompatible with home life simply because they didn't *have* a home life.

■ Then there's a new breed of family in which both husband and wife have agreed to pursue careers that are incompatible with home life. These couples have relegated home life to the nannies, pizza-delivery persons, and professional housekeepers that enable Mom and Dad to continue careening wildly toward the next promotion, paycheck, or emotional high that comes with being intoxicated with one's career.

An article in *New York* magazine profiled four such couples whose marriages, according to the article, "seem to be working."

Wendy and David are both lawyers and parents of a four-year-old daughter. The article states that Wendy and David have "hired a baby sitter and a housekeeper in addition to the nanny, and instituted a regimen that minimizes interference with their work." The couple has been known to take separate vacations, and while one spouse comes home at 6:00 P.M. to relieve the nanny, the other will put in overtime at the office until 9:00, 10:00, or later. Wendy says, "It's hard, but obviously we love it."

Yet both admit "there are times they find themselves longing for each other." One evening, David and Wendy got together with friends and the conversation turned to sex. According to the article, several married friends were lamenting the fact that, after a while, marital intimacy lacked the "pizzazz of making love with someone new."

"Well," Wendy responded, based on her own hectic lifestyle, "by the time you get around to having those kinds of romantic evenings together, it *is* like being with someone new."[1]

The fact is, for years people have been faced with the choice of how to handle incompatibility between career and home life. And for years, many men and women have made the choice to place career *before* relationships, continuing their passion with the workplace at the expense of loved ones at home.

But just because it happens doesn't make it healthy.

Melita says her sixteen-year-old daughter is always coming home with unrealistic requests: "Mom, can I go to an overnight party at Todd's house?" "Mom, the kids from school are driving sixteen hundred miles to Florida for spring break. Can I go?" "Mom, Lisa's dad is buying her a condo for her sixteenth birthday, and she wants me to move in with her. Okay with you?" "Mom, some kids are holding a car wash to raise money for beer and condoms. Can we take the car down to get it washed?"

Melita's typical response (after "Over my dead body") goes something like this: "If all your friends jumped off a cliff, would *you*? If everybody ran in front of trains and got killed, would *you*? What are you, *crazy*?"

Just because someone else makes a stupid choice doesn't mean we have to, too. If someone is *consumed* with climbing the corporate ladder, they're out of balance, and it doesn't matter if that person is married or single, male or female. Choosing a career that's compatible with a family's particular needs *should* be important to men as well as women. Unfortunately, at this stage women are the pioneers in this area, although a growing number of men are beginning to take a stand for greater balance in their lives.

It takes a lot of courage to be a pioneer. While we pioneers are seeking jobs closer to home, avoiding unrealistic overtime, pursuing flexible hours, or turning down that transfer to another city because it would be too hard on the kids, we still have to face colleagues and bosses who believe we're "wimping out." They might even laugh at us. They might harass. They might become condescending or develop a personal vendetta against us.

And let's be honest. That hurts.

The mommy track: helping moms chart a balanced course— or stopping them dead in their tracks?

Back home Saturday morning, Ann plugged in the coffee pot and pulled a box of frozen waffles from the refrigerator. She felt a tug on her leg and looked down to see Brittney, rubbing her eyes, fresh from the sheets in her Minnie Mouse pajamas.

"Hi, Sweetie. Can you go wake up Daddy? Tell him breakfast will be ready in five minutes."

Brittney padded out of the room, down the hall, and disappeared into the bedroom. Moments later Ann heard squeals and giggles as Rick, rudely awakened, wrought his revenge as the tickle monster.

Before getting out the plates and silverware, Ann removed her briefcase and Rick's from the kitchen table. Then she swept a pile of mail and paperwork off one of the kitchen chairs and onto the counter. As she did, a single sheet escaped and fluttered to the linoleum below. Ann stooped to return it to the pile, glanced at the headline, and groaned.

"I just wanted *one* day to forget about all this," she muttered, staring at the paper in her hands. It was the first page of an article she'd torn from *Business Week* magazine, hoping for a quiet moment to read the article in peace.

With the coffee still dripping, the waffles steaming nicely in the toaster, and Rick continuing the tickle session with Brittney, Ann sighed, sank onto a kitchen chair, and reread the headline: "The Mommy Track: Juggling kids and careers in corporate America takes a controversial turn."[2]

Two paragraphs into the article, Ann stumbled onto a couple lines that sounded too good to be true: "Across the country, female managers and professionals with young families are leaving the fast track for the mommy track. They are searching for new ways to balance career goals and mothering—a human place to stand, if you will, between Superwoman and June Cleaver."

Ann stopped reading and stared out the kitchen window. Not a bad idea, she mused. In fact, it sounded almost good. Okay, okay. More than good. Great.

Suddenly she looked down at the article and shook her head. Winning the lottery sounded like a great idea, too. But that didn't mean it was a likely possibility.

Felice Schwartz fueled an inferno of controversy when she proposed the plan that soon became known as the "Mommy track." Schwartz suggested that employers divide women employees into two groups: *"Career primary"* women, willing to work long hours alongside the men, remaining childless or hiring someone to do the majority of the child raising; and *"Career and family"* women, willing to sacrifice promotions, advancements, and jobs that require travel for special arrangements—like job sharing, tele-commuting, extended leave, or flexible hours—that allow them time for their families.

According to Schwartz, this kind of plan would be good for wives and mothers who are looking for a workable way to balance home life and office life.

It would be good for companies, too. Managers would have a way to keep valuable women employees who might otherwise quit work altogether to stay home with kids. Managers could identify, early on, the women willing to pour themselves wholeheartedly into their careers, much like men have for years, and target these women for the training, promotions, and advancement typically enjoyed by workaholic male counterparts.

Opponents, however, say the dual track is just another way to discriminate against women in the workplace. According to excerpts from the article in *Business Week:*

> Opponents see something insidious: a mommy track, separate and unequal, that will permanently derail women's careers, making them second-class citizens at work and confirming the prejudices of male executives.

> "In most organizations, the mommy track is a millstone around your neck," says Richard Belous, an economist at the National Planning Association. In his recent study of 50 management and professional

women who went part-time, Belous had to promise
anonymity: Participants were nervous that just identifying themselves could hurt their careers. "CEO's
and rainmakers don't come out of the mommy track,"
he warns. "If you go part-time, you're signaling to
your employer you're on the B-team."

Still others claim the mommy track is a great idea but, if
implemented, it will make it more difficult for men to begin
leading balanced lives. An editorial in one women's magazine asked why we should continue to accept the premise
that it's okay for men to give their best to their jobs and not
to their families. The article pointed out that if women's
careers are restructured so they can "be there" for the family,
it becomes more difficult for men to negotiate balanced
work lives on the grounds that their families need them—
and suggested that, instead, men be encouraged to join the
"family force" in the same way women have joined the
work force.

In the *Business Week* piece that Ann saved, author Elizabeth Ehrlich writes:

> The notion of two classes of corporate women, only
> one of which makes it to the top, doesn't sit well with
> Faith A. Wohl, a director of employee relations at Du
> Pont Co. "I'm not sure we should honor lack of fam-
> ily as a criterion and value women who are willing
> to put it aside," says Wohl. She argues that in this day
> of two-earner households, with more fathers taking
> responsibility for home and children, the nature of
> corporate careers has to change for everyone.

The article goes on to report that when a major firm in
Chicago offered a part-time track with the option of returning

to the fast track, one of the first employees to sign up was a new father whose wife had just given birth to twins.

By the time Ann finished the article, the waffles were ice-cold. She tossed them in the trash can and popped in a fresh pair. Then she leaned into the hallway and hollered at Rick and Brittney, "Five minutes, guys! If you snooze, you lose!"

Ann fell quiet during breakfast, watching her family as they ate. Brittney was trying, unsuccessfully, to talk her dad into letting her put a drop of syrup in every square of her waffle. Rick, his brown hair tousled from sleep, nursed his coffee and listened patiently as Brittney explained that her best friend, Emily, got to eat her waffles that way. Even the new baby, nestled in its haven, got in on the act by stirring and fluttering and kicking in Ann's womb.

Despite the family drama being played out before her eyes (and in her body), Ann returned to her thoughts. She had to admit that choosing between several career tracks made sense. It gave a woman choices:

- She could pursue a career pell-mell—and give up any real contribution to family life.
- She could stay home full-time with her family—and give up any real contribution to the workplace.
- She could contribute at home *and* in the workplace by compromising advancement and/or seniority on the job. It might mean working part-time while she raised her kids, or quitting work altogether until the kids were older. But it was possible.

But if the mommy track is such a great idea, Ann wondered, why limit it to moms? Why not let dads in on the secret? And what about singles, or grandparents, or married folk without kids? Why not promote balanced living for *everyone*?

Ann had to admit that a more balanced lifestyle—for mommies *or* daddies—would definitely result in a slower career pace. It could mean being passed on the corporate ladder by guys and gals like Mitch, devoted to their work to the exclusion of everything and everyone else. And it would mean that competing successfully with workaholic colleagues would be nearly impossible. Yet, just because her workmates made decisions to lead unbalanced lives, it didn't mean that Ann—

Her thoughts were interrupted by Rick's voice as he lectured Brittney regarding the disbursement of syrup on her waffles.

"I don't care if Emily does it," he was saying. "Do you have to do *everything* that Emily does? If Emily jumped off a cliff, would you jump, too?"

Ann stifled a smile. Then she gave in and laughed. Aloud.

Rick and Brittney stared.

"What's so funny?" Rick asked.

"Funny?" Ann was still smiling. "Did I say something was funny?"

"You're still laughing. Why are you laughing?"

"I'm not. I mean I am, but . . . it's nothing, really. It's just that . . . well, you have a point. That's all. A really good point. I mean, I was thinking the same thing. And then you said . . ."

Ann was laughing again. Rick threw up his hands. "Aw, forget it," he said, reaching for the bottle of Log Cabin. "Here. Have some syrup."

Notes

1. Dinah Prince, "Marriage in the '80s," *New York* (June 1, 1987), p. 31.

2. Elizabeth Ehrlich, "The Mommy Track: Juggling Kids and Careers in Corporate America Takes a Controversial Turn," *Business Week* (March 20, 1989).

Baker's dozen! Baker's dozen!
Haven't you ever heard of a baker's dozen?

6

Dealing with Stress

I Can Cope. I Can Cope. I Can Cope . . .
As Soon As I Eat This Box of
Chocolate Zingers, That Is.

When the going gets tough . . .

It was 6:40 in the evening when Robyn pulled into the driveway after a particularly grueling day at work. Her boss had missed his plane. Six retailers had called in with complaints about the new sales representative. The delivery problem Robyn had been asked to solve for one of their biggest clients, well, didn't get solved. Just when Robyn thought she had worked out all the bugs, she got a call from the client that afternoon saying another delivery had been missed.

Robyn dragged herself out of the car and negotiated the sidewalk, which was strewn with Ruthie's play dishes and Rachel's Weebles. She took the porch steps slowly, feeling sorry for herself as she went, and reached for the screen door handle.

As the front door closed behind her, Robyn let her purse drop to the floor and stood staring into the living room a full quarter-minute before speaking. When she finally did, her words were clipped.

"Jason, what's Rachel's trike doing in the middle of the living room?"

Startled, Jason looked up from where he was watching TV from the couch. "Oh, hi! Didn't hear you come in. What did you say?"

"I *said*, What's the tricycle doing in the living room?"

"Oh, that. It was starting to get cool outside, so I told Rachel she could ride in here until dinner. She doesn't go fast enough to hurt anything."

"I thought we talked about that. You know what it does to the carpet, and there's still danger to the furniture. I don't care how much she begs or whines—"

"I know. I'm sorry. I guess I wasn't thinking." Jason flipped off the TV with the remote, pushed himself off the couch and met Robyn halfway for a brief kiss. "Okay day at work?" he asked.

"No."

"Too bad. Wanna tell me about it over dinner? The kids are really hungry. You got anything planned?"

"Me? Planned?" Robyn repeated slowly.

Jason walked into the vacant kitchen and turned on a light. "Yeah, you know, to eat. We're starving."

Robyn took a couple of deep breaths and counted to ten. That wasn't long enough, so she counted to twenty. She had to count to fifty before she was confident she could walk into the kitchen and pick up a knife in a manner that was going to further the progress of dinner rather than land her a life sentence behind bars.

Later, after the dishes were done, Robyn halfway wished she had said something to Jason, rather than swallowing her anger (swallowing sandpaper would have been more pleasant). It was time they had a heart-to-heart about the division of work, now that Robyn had gone back to work full-time. Then again, Robyn figured she had only been on her job a couple of months. Maybe, if she were simply patient, Jason would begin to take more home responsibility on his own.

But there was something else bothering Robyn. There had been another incident today she wished she could rewrite. Robyn wished she had stood up to her boss when he accused her of giving him the wrong flight number, a mistake that cost him his flight. She was *sure* she'd read the number correctly over the phone to her boss, and that he'd obviously written it down wrong in his hustle to get out the door in time. But she suffered his reprimand in silence, assuring herself that there was some value in being able to take negative feedback in stride.

By nine o'clock the girls were asleep. Jason withdrew to the study to continue working up a plan to rebuild his sales volume, which had nosedived six months ago when a management split rocked customers' confidence in the company. Robyn, feeling restless, went to the kitchen for some Oreos and milk, then slumped in front of the tube. She tore open the bag of cookies, flipped the station till she found a movie, and determined to forget the injustices of the day. The only time she got up was to refill her glass of milk, which she did three times. When the credits rolled across the screen, Robyn finally stirred to turn off the TV and go to bed.

She wasn't feeling restless anymore. Or concerned about the day's events. But she was probably going to need a little Pepto-Bismol to get to sleep.

As she left the darkened living room, she crumpled something in her fist and tossed it in the kitchen wastebasket as she passed. It was the empty cellophane wrapper from the bag of Oreo cookies.

When the going gets tough, the tough get—compulsive?

Robyn uses food to bury her feelings whenever she's faced with a confrontation or when she starts to feel angry. But food isn't her problem; food is just a symptom of the problem.

Buried in the recesses of Robyn's mind are memories belonging to a frightened six-year-old who watched her parents verbally abuse each other for hours on end. Robyn's mom would yell, her dad would yell, and then curses would fly as the couple slammed doors and flung glassware against the walls.

Sometimes Robyn's neighbors called the police to silence the turmoil in the little two-bedroom home on Woodrow Street. But when the officers left, the torrent of rage hadn't been dispelled. It had, instead, been condensed and concentrated into a bitterly potent silence; compressed into a clenched jawline; focused, with all the destructive force of the midday sun through a powerful magnifying glass, into heated, angry looks passed between the man and woman who had once been lovers.

At that tender age, in that house, caught between those kinds of wars, Robyn had made a promise with the kind of unflinching conviction that only a child can drum up. She would *never* be like *them*. She promised, crossed her heart and hoped to die. She would never, ever, *ever* get angry like that.

Robyn grew up in a dysfunctional family.

Judy Stewart, M.A., an expert in women's concerns, defines dysfunction as *"anything* in a family that disrupts the normal, healthy development of each member of the family." Substance abuse among anyone in the family, physical or sexual abuse, even verbal abuse can cause wounds that require more than the passage of time to heal.

An extremely possessive family can be dysfunctional. So can a family that encourages children to hide, rather than express, emotions. A family ripped apart by a bitter divorce can leave ragged scars, as well.

Experts are now estimating that 95 percent of American adults grew up with some sort of dysfunction in their family, something that hindered their development. Very often, men and women from dysfunctional families find themselves coping with the resulting imbalance with some sort of compulsive or destructive behavior.

Robyn learned to abuse food to hide the imbalances stemming from her rocky childhood. Yet children from dysfunctional homes can grow up into many other things:

- alcoholics
- perfectionists
- drug abusers
- compulsive overeaters
- bulimics
- anorexics
- compulsive spenders

They may find themselves abusing their spouse or children—emotionally, verbally, or physically. They often become addicted to destructive relationships. Or they may find themselves frequent victims of dark depression.

A friend of mine simply couldn't control her anger. Carolyn fought for years to tame a fury that seemed to come from nowhere. After she and her husband had their first child, Carolyn found herself exploding without reason when her toddler spilled his milk or misbehaved. She began to worry about the emotional damage her uncontrolled fury was wreaking on her son. But try as she might, she couldn't find rest from the boiling cauldron within.

One day Carolyn picked up a book dealing with safe child care. One of the chapters in the book dealt with detecting sexual abuse of children. As Carolyn read that chapter, something connected inside her mind. The next day, she began recalling memories that had been stored away, out of reach, for twenty years. They were memories of several boys in her neighborhood, teenage boys, and the sexual liberties they took with Carolyn when she was seven and eight years old.

Suddenly Carolyn's unexplained anger had a source. There was a reason behind the madness. For the first time in her life, Carolyn could stop focusing on the *symptom* of her problem, and start working on the problem itself.

Who ya' gonna call?

Carolyn found a Christian psychologist who could help her explore and resolve the traumatic experiences of molestation in her childhood.

Robyn began to consider attending a support group called Overeaters Anonymous.

Jenny found another source of help for her problem.

"I knew my problem stemmed from my childhood," she remembers. "My parents divorced when I was fairly young, and my mom, my sister, and I were forced to move out of our pretty home and into an apartment in the slum area of our city. Budget? Financial choices? Our choices were whether we wanted to spend an extra couple of dollars a month to upgrade from our twenty-roach apartment to a twelve-roach apartment, or whether my sister and I would get a few new clothes for school. We couldn't have both."

Jenny grew up unsure of herself, wondering where she fit in, and what she really had to offer to herself and those around her. Eventually she began to develop a sense of identity around her love of crafts and decorating. Before long, no one could visit Jenny's country-style home without commenting on her hand-crafted creations and painstaking coordination of wallpaper, borders, pillows, rag rugs, knickknacks, etc. More than once—a lot more than once—friends told Jenny her home should be featured in a decorating magazine.

Yet all the beauty of Jenny's home didn't quell her restlessness. She lay awake at night planning how to rearrange the decor, or what her next purchase or craft would be. In essence, she was out of control, driven by the many deep needs resulting from her childhood hardships. Her decorating wasn't a hobby; it had become an obsession.

Jenny began to pray about the problem, realizing that she was no longer in control of her life. She remembers: "I knew the Bible instructs us to be controlled only by God's Spirit, not by alcohol, drugs, food, lusts, or greed—and not even by a hammer or glue gun. I already knew what the roots of the problem were—a gaping void where a strong self-image should have been. I began to spend a lot of time on my knees, asking God what he wanted me to do about this problem."

The more Jenny prayed, the more she felt God was leading her to go "cold turkey." For one year she would abstain completely from buying trinkets for the house or even personal items for herself. She would wrap up her glue gun and stick it in the back of the highest shelf in the farthest closet. Instead she would find a way to develop her identity in Jesus Christ, spending more time in prayer and God's Word.

Jenny survived that year. It wasn't easy, but it was made possible through a lot of prayer. And at the end of the twelve months, Jenny was free again to buy picture frames, sew curtains, or pick up a new pair of shoes.

But she was free in a much greater sense, as well. She was no longer in secret bondage to a compulsive behavior that had become her way of coping with a troubled past.

It felt great. It felt incredibly, awesomely great.

They say the first step is the hardest. Well, the second step isn't exactly a joy ride at Disneyland.

It wasn't the bag of Oreos that made Robyn take a second look. It was the fact that she began to sneak food when Jason wasn't looking.

She wasn't gaining any weight—probably because she starved herself for several days after every binge. But the fact remained that, as her stress level on the job began to build, Robyn began looking forward to her "fix" of sugar to help her cope. After all, it was easier to down a half-dozen donuts than to confront her boss over his condescending attitude, or confront Jason over anything happening—or not happening—at home.

The final straw came when Robyn dropped by the supermarket one evening after work. She needed to pick up a gallon of milk and a pound of hamburger for dinner. By the time she wheeled her cart through the checkout, she'd added a bag of peanut M&M's, a box of licorice, and an Almond Joy bar to her purchases.

Carrying her bag to the car, she thought about the stockpile of sugar in her arms. She picked up her pace, fumbling with one hand for her keys long before she got near the car.

She got the door unlocked in record time, slid into the driver's seat, and ripped into the grocery bag, looking for the peanut M&M's. She tried to tell herself that she was just hungry before dinner, but she knew it wasn't true. The truth was that she felt stressed out, anxious, and physically exhausted from working full-time at the office *and* full-time at home. The truth was that Robyn needed a sugar fix to help her cope.

Her hands closed on the cellophane bag. Suddenly Robyn froze and stared, wide-eyed, at her death grip on the bag.

She dropped the candy, revved the engine, slammed into gear, and screamed out of the lot.

She had just taken the first step. She realized she had a problem.

The second step was just as traumatic. Robyn found a local chapter of Overeaters Anonymous in the white pages.

On the night of the group's weekly meeting, Robyn pulled into the lot of the church where they met. She glanced at her watch: she was five minutes late.

She tooled her car around the parking lot, wondering how she was going to find the right room, until she spied a man walking from his car toward the building. She pulled alongside, unrolled her window, and cleared her throat. When she spoke, her voice was barely above a mutter.

The man stopped and stared. "What?" he asked. "I couldn't hear you."

"Do you know, uh, where Overeatersanonymousmeets?" Robyn ran the words together until they were barely distinguishable.

The man eyed Robyn with a sudden curiosity. Then he shook his head. "I'm here for choir practice."

Robyn grew beet red. She peered over the dashboard, looking furtively for the parking lot exit. Then she noticed a second cluster of cars near a lighted classroom. She parked near the other cars, took a deep breath, and stepped from her car. She could feel the blood pounding between her ears as she walked the distance from her car to the classroom. She paused just outside an open window, listening to the voices inside. She wanted to be sure she wasn't walking into a curriculum meeting or Lamaze class or something.

She heard a man's voice, and then the shuffle of someone walking to the front of the room.

Suddenly a woman spoke. "My name is Carol, and I'm a compulsive overeater."

A half-dozen voices responded, men and women together: "Hi, Carol." There was warmth in the voices, and a wealth of understanding.

Robyn swallowed hard, squared her shoulders, and walked into the room.

> Look for the signs.
> Then be willing to look for help.
> It all boils down to knowing yourself
> and what makes you tick—
> and knowing how to respond if and when
> an alarm goes off.

According to statistics, there's a pretty good chance that you come from a dysfunctional family or have suffered some traumatic event, such as sexual abuse.

If this is the case in your life, you may have learned to cope with the resulting voids and/or wounds through some destructive and/or compulsive behavior. If you have this kind of bondage in your life—if you are prone to verbal abuse, substance abuse, chronic depression, compulsive spending, uncontrolled anger, perfectionism, eating disorder, inability to confront, inability to express emotions, etc.—then stress will only make things worse. Much worse. And if you are a working mother and/or wife, you're probably up to your eyeballs in stress.

Then again, I probably don't have to tell *you* about stress! If you are combining a career and a family, you know exactly what I'm talking about when I say that, some days, it feels like every possible crisis has been accounted for and there's virtually nothing left that could go wrong in your life . . . if it could go wrong, it already has.

Take, for example, one day in the life of Linda's daughter, Tami. Tami, who is the evening manager of a snack bar at a local bowling alley, is the mother of two preschoolers.

Tami is luckier than many employed mothers: her husband, Mike, is a whiz when it comes to helping with the kids and the house. After putting in a full day running the auto-parts store that is part of a family-owned business, Mike comes home, eats dinner, and sees Tami off to work. By the time she comes home, the kids are bathed and sleeping and the kitchen is clean. Yet even with two adults working this hard to make things run smoothly, snafus are inevitable.

Like the week Tami was expecting relatives for an overnight visit. Two days before the arrival of her aunt and grandmother, Tami was feeling the stress of too many things to do in too short a period of time. She threw a load of wash in the machine, tossed together a quick meal, kissed Mike goodbye, and was running out the door for work when three-year-old Nathan begged to go, too.

Mike drew Nathan back inside and waved to his wife. He pointed Nathan toward a pile of toys, then hurried off to check on the two-year-old crying in the den. Nathan, angry at being thwarted in his attempt to accompany his mother, stomped into the bathroom and found a way to express his dissatisfaction. He flung the toilet seat up . . . which doesn't sound like much of an expression.

Unless, of course, the wooden seat cracks the toilet tank and water floods the house.

Mike heard the noise and came running. When he saw the deluge, he groaned, deposited the boys in a dry spot, and raced into the garage, looking for the wrench he would need to stop the supply of water from outside the house.

In the meantime, the washing machine was chugging away in the utility room . . . when suddenly the hose behind the machine worked its way loose and began spraying water all over the carpet and wall. A stream of water blasted a fuse box mounted too close to the washing machine . . . there was a pop and a flash . . . and the house went dark.

About the time Mike got the water turned off, he realized they had lost all electricity, too. He grabbed the boys, found a phone, and made an emergency call to Tami's work.

By the time Tami got home, there was one more surprise waiting for her. In all the commotion Samson, the family's dalmatian puppy, had slipped into the house. He had gone straight for the den, grabbed a couch cushion, dragged it back into the yard, and proceeded to tear the cushion to shreds.

Now, ladies, I know you will be tempted to think that Linda and I fabricated this story. I assure you that, while we consider ourselves to be creative persons, we could *never* come up with something quite this incredulous. Then again, you may not have any problem at all in swallowing this tale. Chances are, you've had your share of horror-story days.

The point is this. Stress abounds. And whenever we are facing intense pressure—from deadlines, relationships, or even a series of tragically comic household crises—we may be driven to cope in any way we can. Too often, our repertoire of coping mechanisms may include the kinds of dysfunctional patterns mentioned earlier in this chapter. When pressures mount, our defenses drop and we can too easily find ourselves relying on destructive levels of eating, drinking, yelling, gambling, spending, etc., as an outlet for our overwhelmed emotions.

Years ago I received a greeting card from a boyfriend in high school. On the cover it said simply, "Be alert." The inside of the card explained: "This world needs more lerts." Linda and I couldn't have said it better ourselves.

The first step in combating destructive coping patterns is to be alert (that's "alert," not a "lert"). The second step is to seek help: professional counseling; lay counseling from knowledgeable, reliable friends; a support group such as OA, Alcoholics Anonymous, or whatever. The best way to deal with unhealthy behavior of this kind seems to be twofold:

1. Total abstinence from the destructive behavior while
2. Seeking healing for the deeper wounds or imbalance.

■ Through Overeaters Anonymous, Robyn learned how to recognize, and how to abstain from, any kind of compulsive eating. And in the weekly meetings, she was encouraged to explore the fears and the repressed anger that led to her food abuse.

■ With the help of the Holy Spirit, Jenny learned how to abstain from compulsive spending and decorating, while exploring and developing her identity in Jesus Christ.

■ As Carolyn began—through counseling—to recognize and resolve her deep-rooted anger over being molested as a child, controlling her own outlandish temper became a possibility for the first time in her life.

It really all points back to the idea that we are *whole* persons, not just a series of roles or collection of parts. Too many times we're so busy trying to achieve perfection at each of our many functions that we overlook a deep wound or imbalance in a place so foundational that it affects every other part of our lives. After all, it's difficult enough for working women to learn to see past our roles and begin to see ourselves as entire persons. Dysfunctional behavior is yet another way to cloud our view of the whole picture.

It's important to develop a deep awareness of the many facets of ourselves—including those that are chipped or broken from our past, or those that aren't functioning as they should today. Because the whole picture—even if it is chipped or flawed—is far more beautiful than selected segments, no matter how perfect those segments might appear to be.

DEVELOPING
WHOLENESS
AS A
FAMILY

We may owe the children an apology.

7

Priorities

*What Working Changes
about Your Role at Home—
and What It Doesn't*

Something's gotta go.

The guests began arriving around one in the afternoon, each sporting a brightly wrapped package and a card with some version of the message, "Happy Birthday, One-year-old!"

Jenny greeted everyone at the door, kissing her parents and hugging Uncle Leonard and Aunt Rooney. While relatives crooned over birthday boy Mathew, Jenny rushed back into the kitchen to finish setting out cold cuts. A moment later nearly everything was ready. Jeff had arranged extra chairs around the kitchen table, the balloons looked great, the punch was ice-cold, and the tea kettle was whistling. But Jenny's homemaker image bit the dust when she pulled the butter tray out of the refrigerator and remembered the finger gouges contributed by one of the kids in her home day care.

She still winces as she tells the story.

"It was the last stick of butter. I was devastated. Such a silly thing, fingerprints in the butter. But a part of me kept asking, 'Would Mom serve gouged butter? Would Aunt Rooney?' That single, deformed stick of butter suddenly symbolized all the little details that have been falling through the cracks ever since I started the day care. As hard as I try, I just can't keep up like I think I'm supposed to."

Jenny sliced the butter restaurant-style, reshaping the gouged pats the best she could. But it'll take more than quick work with a butter knife to reshape the dent she suffered in her self-esteem that day.

Let's face it. Subtracting eight to ten homemaking hours from every day makes a difference in our family life. And it's not a small one.

I'll never forget one sultry July afternoon when I picked Kaitlyn up from Jenny's day care. After the other kids were gone, I stuck around to chat with Jenny while Kaitlyn and Mathew played. The oscillating fan on the kitchen table droned as Jenny and I chatted.

Just then Jeff arrived home from teaching a music class at a local college. He grunted a greeting our way, dropped his briefcase into a chair, and went straight for his tie. "Gotta' get this stuff off," he mumbled, sweating as he tugged at his pullover sweater once the tie was gone.

"I can see why. You're dressed pretty warm for July," I said.

He stopped struggling out of his clothes long enough to peer over the rim of his glasses at Jenny. Jenny looked at me and grimaced. "There were no shirts ironed this morning, and no time to do it, so he had to wear a sweater to cover the wrinkles."

Suddenly I laughed. Passionately. No, hysterically.

Jenny and Jeff stared. Jeff, his face still beaded with sweat, finally said, "Well, I certainly don't see the humor."

"Guess what Larry wore to school today?" I finally gasped.

Jeff shook his head. "What?"

"A pullover sweater!" I said. "No clean shirts. We haven't had time to do laundry in two weeks!"

Jenny beamed. "Jeff, now you know one of the reasons I love hanging around this woman!"

The facts are inescapable. Working full- or part-time changes things at home. Yet too often we pretend nothing's changed. We try to go on performing at home as if we had all the time in the world, refusing to make any compromises or to let go of any standard, thereby failing at every turn. We're like the proverbial monkey who, clutching a nut inside a bottle, can't withdraw his fist because he won't let go of the nut (as a result, he loses the nut *and* his freedom, waking up one morning next to a plastic banana tree at the San Diego Zoo).

Sometimes, in order to save the things of greatest value, we've got to prioritize from one to ten, letting go of the items at the bottom of our list. We've got to let go of the nuts.

If we accept the fact that some things
are *going* to change, we can choose
which things we're willing to compromise—
and which things we're not.

Robyn stood outside the door to the spare bedroom where Jason had a home office and took a deep breath. After attending Overeaters Anonymous meetings for two months, Robyn knew the importance of facing her feelings rather than eating them away.

Nevertheless, confrontation takes time to learn. It also takes practice. And guts. Standing outside Jason's door, gearing up for The Big Talk, Robyn wished she were a million miles away. On a desert island, maybe. With a couple of quarts of ice cream and a bag of Oreos.

She shook the intruding thoughts away and concentrated on the matter at hand, then opened the door.

Jason looked up from where he sat hunched over the desk. There was a weariness in his face. He smiled at Robyn. "Hi, Babe."

"How's it going?" She approached the desk.

"So-so. I've been penciling out Kenman's offer. Moonlighting's not a bad idea, at least till sales pick back up. And I've always enjoyed electronics. I'd be working nearly every evening and weekend, but I could bring in enough money so you could quit work."

"When does Kenman want your answer?"

"Oh, a couple weeks or so. He'll be applying for the small business loan by then."

"Jason?"

"Yeah?"

"I need to talk to you about something."

"Robyn. You're not. . . . "

Robyn laughed. "Don't worry. I'm not pregnant." Suddenly her smile disappeared and she had to cross her arms to hide her shaking hands. "I'm not very good at this," she mumbled.

"Sweetheart, this sounds serious. Sit down." Jason pulled up a chair.

Robyn felt better sitting down. She forced a smile of thanks. "Jason, it's about the workload here at the house. Now that I'm working full-time I just can't, you know, do everything like I used to." She braced herself for an angry response, just like the kind her parents always gave each other.

"You want me to help more around the house?" Jason asked. There was a defensive edge to his voice.

"Not exactly. Well, yeah, maybe. Oh, darn it, yes. Yes, that's exactly the thing. I thought I could do it all myself, but I can't."

"Robyn, I'm working full-time, too. Plus I'm thinking about taking on another job. What do you want from me? Blood?"

Robyn froze. Maybe she was being silly. Maybe she was being unrealistic. Maybe she was being . . . a wimp.

She cleared her throat. "I . . . I know, Jason. But it's not . . . reasonable to think I can add forty hours of work to my week, and your week is going to stay unchanged. I'm still supposed to handle all the things I did before I began the job. At least you get a break, but I'm working from dawn to dark!"

"C'mon Robyn. It's not that bad . . ."

"Not that bad? You don't realize. Like the other night, you came home from work and watched TV. I came home from work and had to clean the house and prepare dinner. Your day ends at five-thirty. At five-thirty, my second shift begins. And it's just not working out." Robyn took a deep breath. "There. I can't believe I said it!"

Jason's brows knit together in thought. "Maybe you've got a point. It's not something I'm thrilled about hearing, but maybe it makes sense."

Robyn slumped, relieved, in her chair.

Jason added, "Help me figure out what we need to do differently."

"And you'll help?"

Jason nodded. "I'll help."

In the following weeks, Jason took over preparing dinner two nights a week, and putting the girls to bed three nights a week. The bulk of the housework still rested with Robyn, but Jason's contribution made a big difference.

Robyn's adjustment wasn't over. It was hard to watch Jason help around the house. Robyn found herself picking at him for doing things differently than she would have done them. It simply wasn't easy to let go of the tasks. But deep inside Robyn believed she'd made the right decision. And she was thrilled that she'd actually gathered the nerve to discuss the problem with Jason—and that no glassware had flown in the process!

Ann remembers a similar conversation with Rick. In fact, she remembers more than one. Actually, she remembers broaching the subject every week for nearly half a year before reality began to sink in.

Rick's intentions were good. He promised to wash and iron his own shirts. He volunteered to take over the grocery shopping. He agreed to take his own suits to the cleaners on the way to work. But his follow-through stunk.

Reality was simply this: It wasn't going to happen. Rick would never get around to sharing the homemaking, despite the fact that Ann was sharing the income earning. So Ann went to plan B. She began to hire help.

"It's amazing what you can pay people to do," she says. "Cleaning, cooking, laundry . . . Every year at my church, our high schoolers earn money by wrapping Christmas gifts. I provide the paper and trimmings, and they do all the work for a buck a box.

"I finally figured, fine. If Rick doesn't want to help me around here, that's okay. But that doesn't mean I have to do it all, either. And the jobs that neither of us can or will do, we'll pay someone else to do."

Working full-time changes things at home. And unless we want to fail at *everything*, we've got to choose which things we're willing to compromise along the way.

■ Tasks are a good place to start. Shifting some of the workload from your shoulders to your husband's and your kids' is a popular option—among women, anyway. The husbands and kids tend to gripe a little.

For the first several years of my marriage, I refused Larry's offers to help wash the dishes or vacuum the floor. Even though we both held full-time positions, I felt "weird" letting him do the tasks I'd grown up thinking of as women's work.

After Kaitlyn was born and I continued my free-lance writing, I wised up really fast. Unfortunately, my husband was already conditioned through years of bungling on my part. It took some adjustment for me to begin to let go of tasks, and adjustment on his part as he found himself roped into jobs he hadn't volunteered for since 1981.

■ Dollars are another alternative. Letting go of the dough can buy you the help you need—especially if your kids and/or husband aren't ready and willing to expand their horizons on the home front.

■ Cleanliness is another "optional" feature for working women. As we've mentioned before, national disaster areas are out. But the lived-in look is in. As a working woman, you have neither time nor energy to fight every war. Choose your battles carefully. Dust and occasional clutter won't kill anyone, and they'll always be there, waiting to be conquered, when your family's grown and gone.

■ Gourmet meals are another candidate. Without endangering the health of your family, remember: You don't have to cook like your mother-in-law does.

Now, Linda and I will be honest with you here. Letting go of tasks, dollars, cleanliness, or four-star meals isn't always easy. But if you make the choice to make your changes in skin-deep areas like these, you'll have the energy and time it takes to preserve high standards where it counts: in the heart of family life.

What working *doesn't* change about your role at home: Taking greater ownership of the quality of life of your family.

Women are the heart of the home. For whatever reasons—social, biological, psychological, cultural, historical, theological—women are the very heart. Putting in the hours to bring home a paycheck changes a lot of things, but it doesn't alter this simple fact.

Linda and I have batted around the idea that if wives put in equal time at the office, their men should have equal ownership of responsibilities at home and with the kids. Fifty/fifty in the career world, fifty/fifty on the home front.

It's a nice theory. And believe me, I'd like it to be an obtainable goal. But it's not.

Consider the world of business. Any corporate consultant would inform you that no effective partnership is run that way. Even in the most intimate partnerships, respect might be split fifty/fifty. Rewards can be fifty/fifty. Work load *should* be fifty/fifty. But two people never share *equal ownership* of the same responsibility. If they did, it would be too easy for each partner to assume that the other had fulfilled some important task. Things slip through the cracks that way.

In most families, wives don't share equal ownership of the financial responsibility to support the family. We may well put in as many hours at the office. We might even be earning more money. But chances are, our husbands feel the heavier burden as the watchdogs of our financial security.

Likewise, one adult needs to take greater ownership for the quality of life on the home front. Husbands of working wives *must* become more involved in the lives of their kids and in the running of their household, but, when it's all said and done, one adult needs to coordinate the family as a working team. This doesn't reduce the need for dad and/or the kids to be strong team players; it actually enables them to be effective.

A pregnant attorney quoted in *Parents* says, "Sure my husband helps out. He says, 'Just *tell* me what to do and I'll do it.' All the managing, meal planning, appointment making and crisis intervention still falls on me. Frankly, I'm better at it, but it still takes *time*."[1]

In the vast majority of families, women are the watchdogs of the home front; women set the tone and atmosphere in their marriages and in their homes.

Consider the fact that women buy 90 percent of all self-help books on marriage and relationships. In most cases, when couples seek marriage counseling, the woman is the mover and shaker behind the decision to get help.

Who keeps the extended family together by planning all the birthday parties, buying birthday and Christmas presents, and hosting holiday gatherings? Mothers. And it's no accident that mothers seem to have a greater primary bond with their children than do dads.

"A mother is prepared at birth biologically to be the primary caretaker," explains Dr. Keith Edwards, dean of Biola University's Rosemead School of Psychology. "There is a partnership grounded in the mother's own biology, even at the hormonal level, that allows her to bond with her child. She often has an intuitive sense of her child's well-being and, even in holding the child, a sense of matching. A child is familiar with his mother's biological rhythms."

He goes on to add that the father's role is no less important. In fact, it's Dad who begins to draw the baby "out of his mother's orbit," as Dad becomes another object that helps the child to differentiate himself from his mother.

But it's no wonder that moms typically provide the primary bond that kids need to thrive. And it's no wonder that women make the home.

There's a second thing your job shouldn't change: Being at the right place and making every moment the right time.

At precisely 2:30 Christine gave Mrs. Feinberg her medication, just as she'd done every day that week. "You're all set for another two hours," Christine told the elderly patient. "Dr. Nickelson will stop in to see you sometime this afternoon."

"Is he the young one? The good-looking one?" Mrs. Feinberg grumbled.

Christine nodded.

"He's too young." Mrs. Feinberg scowled. "What is the man, an intern?"

"No, ma'am. Been on staff since 1979. He's one of County's best." Christine glanced at her watch. "Anything else, Mrs. Feinberg?"

The old women caught the gesture. Her voice softened. "You gonna call your kids now?"

Christine nodded. "They're probably getting home from school right now. I'm off work at three, but I still try to call the boys right after they arrive."

"What do they call it these days? Lock-up kids or something like that."

"Latchkey children. It's when the kids come home to an empty house after school."

"*Hmmpf.* Well, you're a good mother, dearie. What's that commercial? The telephone is the best thing since being there, or something like that."

Christine smiled. "Oh, something like that."

Five afternoons a week, Christine phones home by 2:40. She leaves the hospital roughly half an hour later and stops to pick up Paulie from day care. By the time she pulls into the driveway, her eight-year-old, Sean, is usually perched at the kitchen window seat, watching for her. Twelve-year-old Justin can be found somewhere in the house reading comic books, playing with his Teenage Mutant Ninja Turtles, or watching the Nickelodeon channel on cable TV.

"In the afternoons I try to get a lot done," Christine says. "I catch up on laundry, do the breakfast dishes, and, occasionally, prepare a meal that doesn't come from a box. I've got things pretty well organized. You have to, when you work full-time.

"But I'll never forget the afternoon I was rushing to paper the last wall in the bathroom before Dan got home. Suddenly a tow-headed eight-year-old appeared in the doorway. There were tears streaking Sean's face, and he was holding the hamster. I groaned. The furry little rodent couldn't have picked a worse time to die. I had less than an hour to finish the bathroom.

"When Dan arrived home an hour later, there was dried wallpaper paste on the bathroom wall and a straightedge, X-Acto knife, sponges, and yardstick on the tile floor. But there was this fresh mound of dirt in the back yard. There was a cardboard tombstone, and a bouquet of weeds. And there was this eight-year-old kid, who didn't feel as if he'd lost a mom as well as a hamster."

Listening. Loving. Laughing. Touching.

Teaching. Praising. Tickling. Scolding.

Disciplining. Modeling. Wiping runny noses and tiny rumps.

Treating small hurts with Bactine, and big ones with a balm made up of a piece of your own broken heart.

These things take time. They can't be scheduled onto a calendar or programmed into two hours of "quality time" between dinner and bath time. Our families need to know they are more valuable than our projects. And the only way they learn that is by coming out on top now and then when there's a conflict in scheduling.

It's called flexibility. It's called priorities. Sometimes it's called sacrifice.

My dad often bemoans the fact that, as a self-employed businessman, he was too busy for long family vacations when we kids were growing up. He never showed us the Grand Canyon, he says with deep regret. We should have accomplished more things as a family.

These words always amaze me, because I remember a busy man who was never *too* busy. I remember a man who called the Downey public school system to announce that his girls weren't coming to school that day—the family was going to brunch instead. I remember a man who, more than once, canceled his business appointments and spent the entire day sitting in the living room with a rebellious teen, hashing out the issues until the conflict could dissolve in a hug. I remember a man who scolded a chubby thirteen-year-old for eating a piece of candy before breakfast—and when he saw his words hurt me, showed up hours later bearing a box of See's Candy Nuts and Chews, with the inscription, "I may be a little 'nutty,' but I love you." Even when time was scarce and things got hectic, I knew where I stood. And it was pretty high on the list.

We women can't do it all. But we *can* turn a house into a home, a collection of cohabitating bodies into something called a family. And it's not through designer decorating, spotless cleaning, or a million other things we could "do."

According to Christine, we can do all the "right" things: We can phone our latchkey kids after school. We can join the PTA. We can enroll in weekend crafts with the ten-year-old, or Tuesday night tumbling with our toddlers. We can schedule "dates" with each child. We can read all the books, compare notes with our friends, and turn "being there" for our kids into a precise scientific process that functions on our terms.

But it doesn't mean a thing if we can't toss it all aside at the drop of a tear.

With the pace of living zooming and stress and pressures looming, make time to listen to your family with your heart.

Larry and I sat exhausted in front of the boob tube. We'd just come out of the hectic week I mentioned in chapter 4. (Remember the week he had a bunch of speaking engagements and I had a major writing deadline? Remember the week I sprayed Raid on the dirty dishes instead of washing them?)

Anyway, I had been vegetating in the company of the Cosbys for a good fifteen minutes when a subtle, gnawing anxiety began to well up inside me. I cocked my head and listened to the random noises of our neighborhood settling into nightfall.

A car door slammed somewhere in the distance.

Our refrigerator motor kicked on.

A dog barked in the twilight.

A settling floorboard creaked somewhere in the house.

From our TV, a studio audience burst into raucous laughter at some one-liner Bill Cosby had emitted.

Suddenly I turned to Larry. "It's too quiet."

"You want me to turn it up?"

"I don't mean the TV. I mean Kaitlyn."

I pushed myself up from the floor and peered throughout the house looking for my daughter, who was then three. I found her on the floor in the bathroom, surrounded by strips of peach and blue wallpaper peeled fresh from the wall.

She looked up at me and smiled. I looked down at her and smoked, my anger nearly hot enough to set the fire alarm buzzing.

"Kaitlyn Rose!" I shrieked. "Look at what you did! I can't believe you did that! Don't you remember the spanking you got the last time you pulled that trick? You *know* you're in trouble now. I can't believe—"

Kaitlyn stopped me dead in my tracks with one word. Still smiling up at me, she said the *F* word.

Now, she had no idea what it meant. But several weeks earlier, when she had first repeated it after watching her favorite Tom Hanks movie, *Big*, I'd explained that it was a word our family has chosen not to say. And she had never said it again.

Until now.

Watching me carefully with big brown eyes, she said the forbidden word again. I dropped to my knees on the bathroom floor, amid the shredded wallpaper, and leaned, face to face, toward my daughter. I'd gotten the message. And it didn't have a *thing* to do with wallpaper or language.

"What are you doing?" I said softly.

Kaitlyn just watched me, still waiting to see if I'd heard her. I mean, *really* heard her.

"Did you know I would spank you for this?" I fingered the shredded wallpaper.

Kaitlyn nodded, still watching me carefully.

"And did you know I would spank you for saying that word?"

She nodded again.

"Kaitlyn, *are you trying to get my attention?*"

She nodded a third time. She looked relieved.

I sighed and slumped against the wall next to Kaitlyn. "Okay. First things first. You understood that I would spank you for the things you did. You were right. I'm going to. Right now. And then we're going to talk."

After a brief spanking, I held her in my arms and got to the real root of the problem. I asked her how she felt when Mama and Daddy got too busy for her. I gave her a choice of several words, including *happy, sad, angry, bored.* Kaitlyn picked *angry* and *sad* to describe her feelings.

"Sweetheart," I said, "next time you feel that way, use those kinds of words to tell Mama. Just say, 'Mama, I'm angry.' Or, 'Mama, I need love.' Don't tear things up or use bad words."

Kaitlyn nodded as if she'd learned a lesson. Maybe she had. But not near the lesson she'd just taught me.

Learning to meet needs where they really are— not just where you *think* they are.

Let's face it. We can't afford to misread messages from our families. Kids whose real needs go unnoticed are headed for troubled teen years, and perhaps even time spent on the couch or behind jail bars. Husbands who find themselves misread and misunderstood may find themselves "compensating" in another woman's arms, or addicted to the ecstasy and agony of being a workaholic. And we who simply take communication at face value—never taking the time to listen for deeper messages—can find ourselves wasting valuable time and effort, while still leaving loved ones' needs unmet.

When we interviewed women's concerns expert Judy Stewart for this book, she talked about the importance of looking below the surface to find the deeper need. She gave an illustration of a working woman who didn't have the time to bake the gourmet cookies her daughter had requested for her Brownie troop. Judy suggested that, in a situation like this one, "the working mom may need to ask, 'So what's the real issue here? Does my daughter want me to show off my abilities to bake so that she'll feel good about herself, or does she just need some cookies?' "

Judy went on to say that a working mom shouldn't kill herself finding two extra hours she simply doesn't have in order to bake cookies that aren't meeting any need other than feeding gastric juices in a half-dozen adolescents. Let Nabisco do that.

But if a child needs something to help boost her status among peers or to help her fit in, then that's an important need to be addressed. At that point, the important thing isn't baking the cookies, but meeting the need, which might be addressed by:

- Squeezing out the time to bake the cookies
- Having the daughter help bake the cookies
- Asking Dad to bake the cookies
- Providing a different status symbol that takes into consideration Mother's schedule and *her* need not to be greasing cookie sheets at midnight.

Judy added, "What is the child *really* asking for? What is the husband really asking for? The same goes for employees, employers, friends. Once we find out what the real need is, we can look for creative alternatives in meeting those needs."

And it all starts with listening.

Really listening.

For married women: Giving wholeheartedly as a woman and mother— without demanding equal time *in equal ways* from "Mr. Mom."

"I'll be honest with you. We've had more than *one* fight about it," Ann admitted over lunch at Marie Callender's. Six months pregnant, she had dragged me to the famous pie shop in the wake of an intense craving for their potato-cheese soup. I had agreed to go with her because I, too, suffer frequent cravings for that particularly tantalizing dish, and I'm not even pregnant.

"And how did you resolve it?" I asked. "Or did you?"

"Oh, we did. Eventually. But it wasn't easy. I told you before, I could never get Rick to pitch in fifty-fifty with the housework, right? Well, I guess I figured if he couldn't do his share of laundry, he darn well better take equal responsibility with Brittney."

"And he didn't?"

"Oh, he did. *That* wasn't the problem. He took on half the parenting. But he did it like, well, a father. He didn't do it like *I* would have done it."

"Larry's the exact same way!" I confessed. "He'll help with Kaitlyn, but somehow all the little details get left up to me. He puts her to bed in her clothes instead of her pajamas. He forgets to brush her teeth no matter how often I remind him.

He loves her to death—there's no question of that. But there's just something missing. . . . "

Ann shook her head. "And I thought Rick was the only one."

"So what happened? How did you change him? Bottle the formula and I'll buy a case."

Ann pursed her lips in thought. "That's the thing. I didn't change him. Oh, I tried hard enough. I wanted everything perfectly equal. I couldn't stand the thought of him falling short of my standards of care for Brittney. I couldn't stand the idea that I was still covering more than half the responsibility. We fought about it a lot. And then one day it hit me. We *can't* contribute equally. We're each gifted in different areas!

"I can offer Brittney things Rick simply can't," Ann added. "I know her moods, her tones of voice, her special fears. I even hold her differently than Rick does. She seems more relaxed in my arms than in his. And I've got the eye for details that he doesn't. Maybe it's just because I've had more practice. Maybe it's genetic. I don't know. But I'm better at, well . . . " She floundered for the right word.

"Mothering?" I suggested.

Her eyes lit up. "That's it. Mothering."

"So what did you do?" I asked. "Did you give up asking Rick to help with Brittney?"

Ann looked surprised. "Not at all! I just quit expecting him to do *my* job. As a mom, I mean. I'll always have certain qualities and skills that he'll never have. And that's okay. I can accept that now. It'll never be equal. He'll never do half my job.

"But I'll never do half of his. Brittney needs a mom *and* a dad. Rick's more involved, all right. But using *his* gifts, without releasing me from using the gifts I offer as a woman. And I'm learning that Rick offers her things I never could."

"Like what?"

"He seems much more in tune with Brittney's special skills. Rick's the one who first noticed her love for music. He worked with her for weeks when we took the training wheels off the bike. And he patched her skinned knees the first time—no, the first couple times—she fell out of the tree house."

"Don't they do something on Saturdays?" I asked. "A date or something?"

"Sundays," Ann said with a smile. "Every Sunday afternoon. Ice cream at Thrifty's. It's a tradition now." The smile clouded for less than a heartbeat. It was replaced with a grimace of resignation.

"Okay, okay. So he *does* forget to take her sweater. . . . "

There's something to be said for equality, but not at the expense of who we are as women—or who we are as mothers.

As my writing schedule doubled in preparation for this book and others, I found myself wanting to divide my "mothering" in two, handing Larry one half and saying, "Your turn." But everytime I tried (can I be honest here?) he just didn't cut the mustard. Not by my standards, anyway.

- When Kaitlyn wants to play house, I coo to her dollies. Larry gives them imitations of the Three Stooges.

- When I put Kaitlyn to bed, I impart a kiss, a firm good-night, and leave the room despite her many pleas. Larry keeps her company by falling asleep in a chair next to her bed.

- When I take her outside in winter, I bundle her up till she can rest her arms at shoulder height. When Larry takes her outside, we're lucky if her hair is combed.

I'm gradually learning to accept this simple fact: My husband is not a mother. And that's okay. Because I am.

Holding down a job changes a lot of things, but it doesn't change the fact that there are some things we do—for our husbands, our kids, the quality of our home life—that simply can't be neglected, purchased, subbed in, delegated, relegated, pawned off, or postponed.

When our lives seem overbooked between home and office, it's really easy to want to split our responsibilities as "mom" right down the line, asking our families to absorb the loss.

The fact is, our families can handle half a housekeeper. They can survive with half a cook. They can even get by with smaller portions of chauffeur, interior decorator, outdoor landscaper, calendar secretary, and chief bottle washer.

So what do our jobs change about our home life? On the surface, it feels like *everything*. Suddenly we may have to choose which of our many functions we can still give our families—and which functions we can't. Yet our families can survive with less of what we *do*. They just can't get by with less of what we give them out of who we *are*.

What do our jobs leave untouched? Maybe we can't "do it all." But we can still give our families our hearts. We *can* turn our houses into homes, our families into, well, *families*. And one of the ways we can do it is by cherishing, not relegating, our special place as women, wives, and mothers in our homes.

Notes
1. Gay Sheldon Goldman with Kate Kelly, "Choices of the Modern Mother," *Parents* (October 1988).

I keep telling you, Mom, if I had my own
Nintendo and entertainment center, you wouldn't
need day care.

8

Guilt

The Common Denominator

We don't have enough time,
enough energy, or enough patience.
But too often we've got enough guilt
to furnish an army.

"Is the food in the car?" I asked.

Larry nodded.

"And did you get Kaitlyn's toys for the sandbox?"

"Naturally."

"I set the blanket out, too. Did you get the blanket? Is it in the car?"

Larry laughed. "You're so paranoid. Yes, yes, yes. Everything's in the car. Can we go now?"

"I guess. I just hate that nagging feeling that I've forgotten something."

Larry locked the door behind us. Halfway across the driveway, I turned to him. "Where's Kaitlyn?"

Larry shrugged. "I thought you sent her out."

"Of course not. I thought you were putting her in the car seat!"

We marched back to the house, unlocked the door, and got our daughter.

On the way to the park, we stopped and picked up the Sunday paper. Later, lying on a blanket, hearing Kaitlyn's squeals as Larry pushed her on the swing, I thumbed through the newspaper for the most informative section, the one from which I draw much of my research as well as my philosophy on life: the Sunday comics. I wasn't disappointed.

Three-quarters of the way down the second page, I found something that made my day. The first window showed a kid busily making something with cardboard, crayons, and string. In the next frame she lifted some sort of sign around her neck. Then she walked across the room, past the chair where her father sat reading a book, and on into the kitchen. There at the kitchen table sat Mother, poring over reams of paperwork from the office.

The next frame showed the kid standing in front of the table, staring at her mom. The sign around the girl's neck was visible now. It read: "I'm Cindy. Remember me?" The look on the mother's face was priceless. It was the wide-eyed, crooked-brow grimace of an obviously overworked woman experiencing a motherlode of guilt.

As the kid walked back through the living room, a smile on her face, her dad looked up from his book. "That was sort of cruel, don't you think?" he asked.

The girl shook her head. "Naw, that was just Mom's weekly fix of guilt. It really gets her adrenalin pumping. How do you think she would function without it?"

I brushed a picnic ant off my leg and refolded the newspaper. I also made a mental note to cut out the cartoon as soon as I got home. I figured it would be great to get permission to reprint it in this book.

Two days later, I asked Larry what happened to the Sunday paper. He shrugged. "I think I threw it out."

"Oh, sheesh," I groaned. "I knew I should have torn it out right when I saw it. "

"What? Torn what out?" he asked.

"A comic strip I wanted to use for the book."

"So go get it. It's probably in the trash can right now."

"I can't," I moaned. "I threw greasy chicken bones and watermelon rinds in there. The thing's a slopping mess. It's lost. It's lost! I'm such a blunderhead. If I weren't such a procrastinator, if I would just follow through with things at the time, this never would have happened. What a screw-up!"

How ironic that something as simple as losing a cartoon strip on guilt could make me feel so guilty.

Guilt: The tie that binds.

If Christians share a bond based on their common commitment to Jesus Christ . . .

If Hare Krishnas are identifiable by the shared feature of shaved heads and a wax drip on the forehead . . .

If Batman Fan Club members are united by their mutual devotion to the masked winged wonder . . .

Then working mothers share a bond of crushing, debilitating guilt.

Barbara Berg, writing for *Ms.* magazine, says:

> After two years of interviewing nearly 1,000 women of varying backgrounds across the nation, I learned that guilt was their greatest emotional problem. My findings both saddened and surprised me. It saddened me to realize that the present generation of working mothers, the beneficiaries of so much hope and striving, were haunted by such conflict. "The guilt feels deep and almost physical," was how one mother put it, while another labeled it "the most painful experience of my life."[1]

A couple of years ago, I spent two hard weeks finishing up a manuscript for another publisher. For those two weeks, Kaitlyn was shuffled between the homes of friends and relatives as I pounded the computer at a frantic pace.

On a Friday morning, the finished manuscript was just hours old. I was supposed to leave the house by 9:00 A.M. to make a two-hour drive to Palm Springs to deliver my masterpiece. At 8:30 I went to wake Kaitlyn, get her dressed, and drive her to Jenny's house.

Before I kissed her awake, I looked down at my sleeping cherub and felt guilt pangs strong enough to short-circuit a pacemaker. I went straight to the phone, called Jenny, and told her Kaitlyn wasn't coming that day. Then I dialed my mom's house and asked if she were willing to take a scenic drive through the desert; we could spend the drive-time visiting, and she could play with Kaitlyn while I met with my editor.

The day went like clockwork. Everyone had fun. I met my deadline. And my guilt was assuaged.

But if you're a working mother, you already know that solving the "Big G" is rarely that easy.

Guilty, one and all.

Melita pointed to the bottom line on the loan application. "Your John Hancock there, and we're all set."

The customer picked up a pen and leaned over the form. As he was writing, Melita continued, "You'll need to keep a copy of that first sheet I gave you, because it lists—"

She was interrupted by the phone.

"Excuse me." She smiled, then picked up the receiver. "Melita Sorenson. Can I help you?"

"Mom, it's me," a voice said breathlessly.

"Hi, Brenda," Melita said evenly. "I'm with a customer at the moment. I'll need to call you right—"

"Mom, wait!" Brenda blurted out. "I'm calling from the school office. The bus is leaving in five minutes. You were supposed to bring my cheerleading uniform, remember? Did you bring it? The secretary says she can't find any bag or *anything* with my name on it."

Melita's heart plummeted to somewhere near her fallen arches. "Honey, I . . . "

"Mahhh-uuuum!" Brenda wailed. "You didn't bring it! How am I supposed to cheer? You *knew* how important this was to me!"

"I . . . I'm sorry." Melita groped for the right words.

Brenda rushed on. "I *can't* believe you didn't *bring* it. You *said* you were going to bring it. I can't believe this. This is the *worst* day of my life!"

The line went dead with a click, but not before Melita heard the quiver in her sixteen-year-old daughter's voice as she fought back angry tears.

Melita hung up the receiver. Her customer returned her pen. They shook hands, and business continued as usual.

On the surface, anyway.

Below the surface, one loan officer was racked with pain.

The next day, over lunchroom coffee, Melita confided in a friend from data processing. "There's a part of me," she admitted, "that feels it should be enough that I work my tail off keeping a roof over our heads."

"And what about the rest of you?" Peggy queried.

Melita sighed. "The rest of me knows that's *not* enough. I mean, Brenda doesn't have a real dad. It's not fair that the only parent she *does* have has to be a 10-percent mom."

"A 10-percent mom?" Peggy gave a snort. "That's being pretty hard on yourself, don't you think?"

"I don't know. That's how I feel, anyway. I'm not there to talk when she gets home from school. I've missed more parent-teacher conferences than I care to remember. As a kid, Brenda always got those cheapie store-bought Halloween costumes instead of homemade ones. I can't even be there to drop off a cheerleading uniform when she needs it."

Peggy grinned. "My mom always made my Halloween costumes. I always envied the kids who got to wear the store-bought ones."

Melita eked out a smile—a small one. "Thanks. But I still feel miserable." She stirred her coffee. "Pass the creamer, would you?"

Peggy complied.

"Now that's an idea," Melita said suddenly. "Rat poison— in the coffee! I'll bet I wouldn't feel a thing."

"You're feeling good enough to joke. That's a good sign."

"I don't know about that. I hear some people even joke at funerals."

Melita feels guilt over her performance as a parent. Christine, on the other hand, doesn't feel as guilty about her parenting as she does when she invests a little time or energy in herself.

"Maybe it's because of my job," she says. "As a nurse, I'm a caregiver. I give all day long. And then at home, I take care of Dan and the kids and the house and my dad, who lives a couple miles away but has a hard time getting around these days."

Christine continues with conviction in her voice. "And I'm good at what I do, too. I'm good at sensing other people's needs and knowing how to respond. One of our doctors, Nick Nicholson, says I'm one of the best on staff."

Christine twists a strand of red hair around one finger as she thinks. After a long pause, she finally adds, "The only person I have a hard time taking care of, I guess, is me.

"Every time I take a couple moments for myself, I feel incredibly guilty, like I should be doing something for Dan or reading to the boys or baking something for the nursing staff or the Cub Scout troop or something. I've been feeling this way for so many years, sometimes I wonder how it would feel to feel good about myself again. I really can't remember what those days were like anymore."

Ann feels tremendous guilt over the amount of time she's away from home. "Some days Brittney changes hands three times before I can get home to her," Ann laments. "I drop her off at kindergarten in the morning, and a college student picks her up and brings her home. But three days a week, the student has to leave for class before I can get home, so my mom drives over and subs in. Then there are the nights I'm out of town, have to work late, or am at some PR event. On those nights Rick puts her to bed, and I don't even see my daughter until I drop her off at school the next morning."

Finally, Robyn winces as she recalls one of her sources of major guilt: "My church. Definitely my church. I mean, it's not like anyone comes out and says, 'You're sinning,' but the message comes through in subtle ways. Like the women's fellowship and luncheon always being held on Thursday morning. Like the emphasis on home-baked items at our after-glows after evening services. Like sermons where any illustrations of women, other than homemakers, are conspicuously missing.

"It's as though my church totally ignores the fact that there's even a breed of animal called a working woman. Yet studies done in evangelical churches show that 60 percent of mothers of school-aged children work outside the home. So we're actually a majority.

"In my heart, I can see some real benefits coming from me working. Financial benefits, sure. But I'm also learning things about myself that I never had a chance to learn before. I'm starting to get a handle on my compulsive eating problem, and I'm even learning how to handle conflict better, at home and at work. I had that talk with Jason about him helping out more around the house. I was terrified to do it. But Jason was really easy to talk to, and I discovered the conversation didn't have to escalate into a yelling bout like things always did with my parents.

"So there are some real pluses. But a major negative is the nagging guilt I feel over not living up to the expectations of my church. I'm not even sure they're all God's expectations, but my church sure seems to think so. I've lost status in their eyes; they think I'm really doing something awful. Sometimes I feel I've been banished to an invisible subgroup with invisible needs. And that's really hard to live with."

> Guilt can't be whitewashed or
> swept under the rug.
> If you find that difficult to believe,
> just ask Lady MacBeth.

Guilt is a lot like the chewing gum I give my kindergartner: It pops up in the strangest places. It's also a little like some of the food in my refrigerator: It's not always recognizable.

When Lady MacBeth plotted the murder of her husband's royal rival, she appeared unruffled by the heinousness of her actions—until she started seeing things and roaming the candle-lit castle halls at night, moaning, "Out, out damned spot" (the phrase every high-school English student loves because, let's face it, it's titillating to hear the *D* word read aloud in class).

In Poe's "The Tell-Tale Heart," a murderer was so consumed by guilt that he imagined an incessant heartbeat so loud and so real that it drove him to scream his confession to the first detective he saw.

For working women, the results of living with guilt may not be as dramatic as the preceding examples, but they can be just as disruptive to you *and* to your family. The destructive powers of guilt don't stop at one individual; as you twist and suffer under the heavy hand of guilt, the husband and little ones you love are impacted, too. In order for your "working" family to experience wholeness, the avalanche of guilt you probably live with *must* be resolved.

■ **Discontentment** can be one of the first results of living with guilt. Ann faces this daily. "No matter where I am, I feel as though I'm in the wrong place," she admits. "If I'm at home, I feel guilty over the work piling up at the agency. If I'm at the office working on some campaign, I feel guilty about not spending the time with Rick and Brittney. I can't win."

■ Another outgrowth of guilt is the **inability to give to ourselves.** It makes sense that if a woman feels she's failing on every front, she won't feel much like rewarding herself in any way. I mean, when you're feeling guilty about your kids, guilty about your job, guilty about your marriage, and guilty about the constant lived-in look of your home, who needs yet another dose of guilt for taking the time to read a novel, see a movie with a friend, take on a hobby, or join the gym? After all, *shouldn't* you be using that time for your family?

■ Let's take guilt a step further. We who are unable to give anything back to ourselves are setting ourselves up quite nicely for **burnout.** We give and give and give and give without allowing ourselves anything in return—not even the satisfaction or joy that can come from reaching professional goals or meeting the needs of loved ones. We're always berating ourselves for missing the mark. But even the most guilt-ridden woman has her limits. One day the guilt mill will simply grind to a halt. That woman will either walk away from it all, succumb to deep depression, or take up residence in a padded cell.

- Guilt can have **physical and mental effects**. Living with constant guilt is very stressful, and we all know how damaging long-term stress can be: headaches, backaches, greater susceptibility to colds and flus, depression, heart disease, exhaustion, insomnia—the list could go on and on. One out of two hospital beds in America is occupied by someone suffering ultimately with stress. Living with constant guilt can be our ticket into one of those beds.

- Dr. Sharon Nathan, with New York Hospital at Cornell Medical Center, refers to **anger** as the flip side of guilt. When Robyn finally got up the nerve to ask Jason to help around the house more, she was thrilled at his positive response. But as he began to help wash the dishes, iron his shirts, and give Rachel her baths, Robyn discovered her own response was anything *but* positive! She found herself consistently berating Jason over little things he didn't do "quite right." The more Jason helped, the angrier Robyn felt. It took her a couple of weeks to sort out her feelings, and then she realized she was angry at Jason because she felt guilty. Jason was doing the extra work Robyn couldn't handle, the work that Robyn's church made her feel should be her primary function. Robyn felt like a failure because she couldn't do it all. Her way of coping with that guilt was anger.

Anger takes the focus off our own guilt feelings and places it somewhere else. Guilty anger misdirected at a husband can destroy communication, trust, and sexual intimacy. Directed at children, it can erode their self-esteem and confidence. And guilty anger directed at ourselves can take us right back to an inability to do anything nice for ourselves. After all, why reward someone you're really ticked at?

■ In addition, a guilty mother may be an **indulgent** mother. There's a rather tongue-in-cheek article in *Harper's Bazaar*[2] that gives several reasons why working moms who invest heavily at Toys "R" Us are *not* buying their way out of a guilty conscience. They include: (1) Working mothers don't have time to say no when kids beg for toys. The article states, "You've probably had your fill of negotiation at work. So what happens? You buy the toy." (2) If we teach our kids that spending money is fun, they may be more motivated to earn their own. (3) Other toys (like the "latest toy vaccination kits" or the $219 block set) are necessary to prepare our preschoolers for careers as doctors or architects. (4) Still other purchases are necessary to develop our kids into what we're not: well-rounded adults. Berg writes, "If you feel your career in computers has developed only the left side of your brain, you start Brendan off with *Big Bird Listens to the Orchestra*, vats of Play-Doh, and puppet theatres."

Yet the fact remains that, too often, guilty parents try to compensate with toys, special freedoms, and lack of discipline. Let's be honest: It's hard to discipline an unruly kid when you're convinced *your* failure or absence is at the root of his problems.

■ A final pitfall of living with guilt is something I personally struggle with. And that is **addiction.**

I'm addicted to guilt. Like the cartoon woman on the Sunday comic page, I need a constant level of guilt to keep me moving. I first noticed it when I was pregnant with Kaitlyn. Every morning I would open the kitchen cupboard, stare at my prenatal vitamins and think, *I'll take them later.* But more days than not, I allowed myself to feel guilty rather than pop those two little pills.

The same with plants. I've got a black thumb when it comes to plants. I watch them shrivel away over a period of weeks, reminding myself every day, "You've really *got* to water those plants." They say people should talk to their plants. The thing I say most often to mine is, "Don't look at me like that. I know what you're thinking. Knock it off or I'll turn your pot toward the wall." Now *that's* guilt.

Writing letters to friends is no different. I feel incredible guilt over the fact that I've never responded to 99 percent of the letters I receive from faraway friends. My abstinence from letter writing simply bewilders all my friends and family who continue to write increasingly pointed letters containing words like *one-sided* and *neglect* and *revenge.*

It bewildered me, too, until a couple of years ago. I was trying to lose some extra pounds long left over from my pregnancy. I would make good headway for a couple of weeks, then seemingly sabotage my efforts. Over and over again, I hit the two-week mark and then went food-crazy. I couldn't figure it out. Then one afternoon I was mulling over my problem while vacuuming the hallway, when a thought came out of nowhere and hit me like a Mack truck:

If I lost my weight, what would I have to feel guilty about?
Suddenly it all made sense. The prenatal vitamins.
The dead plants scattered throughout my house. The
unwritten letters. The added pounds. Even the incredible guilt I feel over something stupid, like arriving at the park and discovering we left the food,
blanket, sand toys (or Kaitlyn!) at home.

The truth was simple: I was an addict. I was hooked
on guilt!

Guilt is such a powerful emotion that it can become self-
perpetuating. It can become a raw, festering wound that is so
excruciating to the touch it's easier to look the other way and
let the infection rage, rather than braving the one-time pain
of cleaning and dressing.

Other times, guilt and its ugly companions (including discontentment, burnout, anger, indulgence, self-denial) leave our
self-esteem so ravaged that we begin to feel we don't deserve
anything better. Freedom from guilt becomes a gift we refuse to
give ourselves. And just to make sure we don't accidentally feel
better, we may subconsciously find ways to replenish our guilt
level like I did with the vitamins, plants, and letters.

They say an alcoholic can experience such crushing guilt
over his or her addiction that the only way to numb the pain
is to plunge even deeper into the mire of drunkenness.

For *anyone* consumed by guilt, the cycle is vicious. But it
can be broken.

Step One: Face your feelings.

One night after dinner, Robyn sat at the kitchen table, watching Jason with a critical eye. He had just stepped to the sink
with an armload of dirty dishes.

Robyn felt like a schmuck, sitting there, watching her husband do *her* job. But for the first time she didn't lash out at the way he left the water running too long or used too much Palmolive. For the first time, rather than camouflaging her feelings with misdirected anger, Robyn just sat there and felt guilty. It felt worse than she ever could have imagined.

Just then Ruthie accidentally knocked over an empty plastic cup. It bounced off the table and hit the floor with a smack. Anger welled up in Robyn like a rising tide. But instead of snapping at her six-year-old, Robyn swallowed the impulse and tried to go back to thinking about the *real* problem—her feelings of guilt.

For just a moment, don't run from your guilt. And don't *dare* think about burying the pain under a dumpload of additional guilt. Try not to misdirect it in fury. And please don't buy your way out of it, eat your way out of it, drink your way out of it, or buckle under it in martyrdom.

Just think about it.

What are the issues over which you feel the most guilt? Your child-care situation? Missing your son's Little League games? Feeling too tired in the evenings to do anything with your husband other than watch the eleven o'clock news? Serving microwave meals six nights a week? Raising latchkey kids? Not keeping up with workaholic colleagues in your office? Being too impatient with your preschooler? Getting around to mopping your kitchen floor only during even-numbered months? Forgetting to change the baking soda in the refrigerator? Forgetting to *put* baking soda in the refrigerator?

Whatever their source, your feelings of guilt *must* be dealt with.

Step Two: Time for the hard questions . . . Is your guilt valid?

We live in a society that believes in the abolishment of anything that seems confining or uncomfortable. You know, little things—like morality, unwanted pregnancies, boundaries . . . and guilt.

We already know that boundaries are healthy. Often, so is pain, which is nothing more than our body's way of attracting our attention to a dangerous, maybe even potentially fatal, condition.

Guilt *can* be healthy, too. It can warn us of a deeper problem—the existence of dangerous or even deadly choices. Like the blinking dashboard light signaling low oil, guilt can be a friend, alerting us to something that could disrupt or even destroy our lives. Remember all the results of unresolved guilt? Anger, self-denial, burnout, discontentment, indulgence, addiction? These maladies will seem like a day at Disneyland compared to the havoc wrought by *deserved* guilt gone unheeded.

After you face the *feelings* of your guilt, you have to face the *validity* of your guilt. Is it valid? Are you *really* guilty? If you are unsure, take a look at the following five "nuggets of insight" regarding deserved guilt and see if and how they apply in your life:

1. Deserved guilt requires a choice.

If a phone call makes you burn dinner, if a flat tire makes you late for a job interview, if you spill coffee on your boss's dress, the guilt you may feel is an impostor. Accidents may fill us with regret (and even get us fired!), but they are not appropriate sources of guilt.

Neither are situations you can't control. If you don't have control over something, you're not a candidate for appropriate guilt. Both Melita and Ann feel guilty that their full-time jobs rob them of time with their families. Yet, as a single mother, Melita's full-time job is not a choice; it's a necessity if Melita and Brenda are going to eat and stay warm. Within the confines of that "given," Melita has made every effort to choose time with Brenda over demanding career moves. Her choices have been good ones; maybe it's time she stopped punishing herself for the things she didn't choose.

The competitive pace at which Ann pursues her career *is* a choice. When Ann suffers over the fact that neither she nor Rick are raising their daughter, she knows she holds the power to make things different, and to eliminate her greatest source of guilt.

So that's the first question. Did you make a choice?

2. Deserved guilt accompanies a moral wrong.

- If you're having an affair with the copier repair man, you'd better feel guilty.

- If you're making your career your god, you'd better feel guilty.

- If you're too busy to care that your marriage is teetering at the threshold of divorce court, I sincerely hope the guilt keeps you awake at night until, cotton-headed and bleary-eyed, you agree to reprioritize your life.

3. Deserved guilt comes from doing something that is circumstantially wrong—something that is unhealthy for your family or yourself—even if there is nothing morally wrong with your choice.

There are many choices that may be, in and of themselves, excellent choices. Yet sometimes choices that work well for a neighbor or a colleague or a friend still manage to have a destructive influence in our own lives. Here are some examples:

- Making the choice to leave a child in day care for forty-five hours each week isn't morally wrong. In fact, some children will thrive in this environment. But if your child is miserable and cowering as a result, it's time to listen to your guilt.

- If trying to "do it all" leaves you listless, unproductive, and ineffective at work, then you aren't being fair to yourself or to your employer. Coming in late three mornings a week, writing personal letters between customers, or letting lunches drag repeatedly into work time can provide you with a pretty valid case of guilt. (It can also provide you with a ticket to the unemployment line if you aren't careful.)

- Serving junk food to your family isn't mentioned in the "Thou Shalt Nots" of the Ten Commandments. Nor will it land you time in jail. But if the most balanced meal your kids eat in an entire week is Pop-Tarts and milk, then you probably deserve whatever guilt you're feeling.

4. *Deserved guilt calls us to redemptive action.*

If you are feeling guilty about something over which you have control, and which is morally wrong and/or destructive to you or to your family, then you may well be dealing with valid guilt at some level. If this is the case in your life, there's still hope. Valid guilt is not a chronic condition. You don't have to go on living with guilt. If you've made a wrong choice, unmake it. It's that simple.

The first time I remember destructively screaming at Kaitlyn, she was still in her infant car seat. She was probably a little over a year old, and I have no idea what she was doing to bring on my rage. Dumping the contents from my purse? Monogramming the upholstery with my lipstick? Making paper airplanes from the pages of her new $24.95 book of nursery rhymes?

I don't remember. I just remember getting *really* ticked. So I made a choice. I screamed my head off.

After I pulled to the side of the road and peeled Kaitlyn from the ceiling of the car, I found myself battling the guilts. And the guilts were winning.

I fought in vain through several intersections. Finally, I knew what I had to do. I apologized to Kaitlyn—not for my anger, but for my temper. Then I asked her to forgive me.

There's nothing righteous about knowing you've done something wrong and feeling guilty for hours, weeks, months, or even years. Admit the problem and make amends. Those amends may be as simple as an apology, or as complex as restructuring your entire life. But don't live guilty.

- Having an affair? Get out. NOW.

- Is your career your god? Reprioritize your life, change jobs, or stay home.

■ Are you too busy to save your marriage? Go to *any* lengths to get unbusy. And do it today, or you may find yourself alone tomorrow.

■ If day care is traumatizing your kids, find an alternative, or you'll reap destruction for years to come.

■ Slothful performance on the job is a poor Christian witness, unethical, and destructive to your own sense of self-worth. Without swinging to the equally destructive side of the pendulum called "workaholic," find some way to incorporate integrity into your office performance. If it's literally impossible to do so, your life is overbooked and you may need to cut back (hours on the job, or responsibilities at church or home) to find a manageable balance.

■ Serving junk food to your family? If you want to live to see grandkids (and have your kids healthy enough to bear some), take action now.

5. Finally, deserved guilt, to be completely resolved, demands forgiveness.

After we've done whatever we need to do to set things straight, there's got to be forgiveness.

Sure, we've got to ask forgiveness from anyone we've wronged. And it's desirable, but not imperative, that they forgive us right away. Forgiveness is a process; it takes time. Besides, at that point, their unforgiveness is between them and God.

But the critical, have-or-die forgiveness that we simply *must* obtain is from another source. We've got to learn how to forgive ourselves. If the wrong actions are stopped—and if we've done everything in our power to correct the situation, asking forgiveness of God and others we may have wronged—then our slate is clean. In fact, we have something of even greater value than a totally clean slate. We have something we didn't have before we sinned and repented of that sin: We have wisdom, and we have experienced God's grace.

If we *don't* forgive ourselves, we are wasting both that grace and wisdom. We are neither free to draw closer to God through his grace, nor free to help others through what we've learned.

We simply *have* to let go of the guilt.

Step Three: Accept guilt-free living.

Guilt is not a "must have" trait for working women. We *can* live guilt-free.

If we've been suffering under *deserved* guilt, nothing will feel more freeing than eliminating the cause of that guilt! But what if we flunk the guilt test? What if we . . .

- didn't have a choice,
- didn't do anything wrong,
- aren't hurting ourselves or our families,
- don't have anything to amend,

. . . and we're still crushed by guilt?

Here's what three women chose to do about their "undeserved" guilt:

■ Robyn suspected that she was a victim of undeserved guilt. She examined her choices. She checked her heart for wrongdoing. And she decided she flunked the guilt test when it came to letting Jason help around the house. There was nothing wrong or unhealthy with Jason helping. Instead, Robyn's guilt stemmed from her unrealistic expectations for herself.

Recently Robyn's been trying to adjust her expectations and learning to respect her boundaries. It's not easy. It's a day-by-day decision. And it's going to take lots of practice. But Robyn's willing to work at it, because living guilt-free is worth the effort.

■ When Melita took a long, hard look at the way she spent her time as a single parent, she knew she'd done the best she could with what she had. Some things were simply beyond her power to change. But how could she move past the guilty pain? How could she get past the feeling that she had, somehow, failed Brenda?

When Melita admitted these feelings to her friend Peggy, the other woman squeezed Melita's hand.

"Don't you see, Melita? That's a start. Just recognizing your innocence in that area is a big start."

"But now what?"

"Don't accept the guilt anymore."

Melita groaned. "Easier said than done."

"Okay, okay. Try this. Every time you start to feel guilty, close your eyes and picture the guilt as a pail of water or garbage. Then imagine a window. Then picture yourself picking up that guilt and heaving it out of your life!"

Melita nodded. "Interesting. And it might even work."

Peggy smiled. "Just make sure to imagine a clear sidewalk before you give it the ol' heave-ho."

■ Christine flunked the guilt test, too. The guilt she felt whenever she took a moment for herself was completely unjustified. There's nothing righteous about self-denial or self-punishment. If there was, Jesus' command to love our neighbors as ourselves would take on an entirely different meaning.

Christine dealt with her guilt by practicing, every week, at receiving something from herself. The first week meant allowing herself to read a chapter a day of a favorite novel. During the second week she signed up for a one-hour Saturday class on T-shirt painting. In the third week, Christine asked Dan to watch the boys while she took a brisk walk after dinner every night for five nights.

As Christine, dressed in sweats, headed for the door on the third evening, Dan intercepted her with a kiss.

"Enjoy your walk," he said.

"Thanks!"

Dan turned to leave, then he stopped. "I don't know what's different," he puzzled, "but you've sure been happier lately. And it makes a difference around here. I feel it. The kids feel it, too. Whatever you're doing, I'm just glad you're doing it."

Adjusting expectations. Respecting personal boundaries. Using imaginations to visualize guilt-free living. Practicing every day. These are some of the ways women just like you are learning to cope with unjustified guilt. Because it makes a difference. For us. And for the people we love.

Notes

1. Barbara Berg, "The Guilt that Drives Working Mothers Crazy," *Ms.* (May 1987), p. 56.

2. Dale Burg, "Toying with Guilt: The Art of the Deal," *Harper's Bazaar* (July 1988), p. 110.

But Mom, the Boy Scout campout isn't until
next weekend.

9

Flying Solo

Special Helps
for Single Moms

Is she a masochist?
Does she welcome punishment?
Is she addicted to work, stress, poverty, and guilt?
No! She's a single parent!

A squeal pierced the wall separating the two rooms. Then a grunt. And then a breathless giggle as eleven-year-old Dallas tried to immobilize his sixteen-year-old brother in a headlock.

Linda, staring at her computer in the bedroom, heard a low *thud* as Dallas connected solidly with a piece of furniture in the living room. Linda tried to gauge by the sound if it had been a leg against the coffee table or a head against the wall cabinet. She finally decided it had been a leg against the coffee table; the head and cabinet combination usually made a hollower thud—probably because one of the two connecting elements was virtually empty.

She was thinking of the cabinet, of course.

She tried to refocus her attention on the computer screen, to recapture momentum on the free-lance project that was due next week. But the words flowed about as smoothly as her life seemed to be flowing at the moment. In fact, when she thought of her life, *smooth* wasn't the word that came to mind. She usually conjured up an image of Niagara Falls, the part where trillions of tons of cascading water smash into the churning, angry rapids at the foot of the multistory drop.

A yelp of anger from Dallas snapped Linda back to their two-bedroom apartment in Ventura. There was another scuffle. Another thud.

Muttering, Linda pushed herself from her chair. Roughhousing was one thing; sibling demolition another thing entirely.

All she had to do was walk into the living room, express parental disapproval in mounting decibels for two or more minutes, and she could continue her work in peace and quiet. It seemed like a simple plan. But as soon as Linda stood up at her desk and turned around, she realized she had a problem.

Getting to the living room meant passing the mounds of dirty laundry—piled strategically beneath an open window—and the mounds of clean clothes on the other side of the room, waiting to be folded.

Even worse, thinking ahead, Linda realized that reaching the living room would provide a reminder of even more clutter. The mess had been piling up for two weeks as Linda faced deadlines on two free-lance projects she had accepted in addition to her full-time job. Unfortunately, moonlighting to pay the rent was a necessary evil.

The roughhousing had turned hostile, and Chris and Dallas yelled back and forth. Linda riveted her eyes straight ahead, away from the clutter, and began to push through toward the living room and her frequent referee duties.

Suddenly she detoured into the safety of the bathroom and locked the door. Cold water on the face might help. But it wasn't likely. Deep down, Linda knew it would take more than a reviving splash to solve her problems. She was overwhelmed.

Linda's situation isn't unique. With more than 20 million single-parent families in America today, a significant number of adults face the daily burden of being mother, father, home-maker, and breadwinner, all rolled into one.

Working women who are struggling to raise a family by themselves get no reprieve from the majority of issues discussed in this book, which include guilt, unrealistic expectations, and wearing too many hats without the time or energy to wear them all well.

Then there are the added pressures of missing—among other things—someone to help referee the kids, someone to help pay the rent, someone to help tidy the house. Linda says she realizes the average working mother *with* a husband gets less than half an hour of household help a day from her man. But, as Linda points out, even half an hour is still thirty minutes more than nothing.

One is a lonely number.

According to Melita, the loneliest moments for single parents seem to be those times of great joy or crisis. "When Brenda landed a big role in her seventh-grade play, I was so proud," Melita remembers. "But watching her up on stage, dressed in a pioneer-days costume made out of thrift-store seconds, I also felt alone. It didn't matter that I was sitting in a school cafeteria with two hundred other parents. I wanted to share the memory with someone who was important to me and important to Brenda. But there wasn't anyone. It was just me."

And as for crisis?

Well, Linda knows about crisis. Take the following, for example, which Linda experienced several years ago.

It was 2:46 A.M. when Linda finally threw back the covers and climbed out of bed. She tried to contain her fear as she dressed in the dark. Then she walked across the hall, into the boys' room, and shook her older son gently by the shoulder.

Chris pried his eyes open and stared, unfocused, at his mother.

Linda whispered, "I can't sleep. I'm going for a drive, but I'll be back soon."

Chris struggled to sit up enough to hug Linda's neck, mumbling, "I love you, Mom," before dropping back onto his pillow.

Linda grabbed a sweater from the hall closet and headed toward the front door. Doorknob within reach, she suddenly turned and hurried into the kitchen. She rummaged through the junk drawer for the phone book, then copied down a number. Beneath the number she scribbled the name of her doctor, then tucked the slip of paper in her pocket.

She drove for several miles along deserted roads, dark and eerie in their night hues. Scattered street lamps spilled pools of white, but the shadows were strong that night. Linda looked in vain for some sign of life: another car, a porch light, a window illuminated by the flickering blue glow from the TV of another restless soul.

Suddenly, she clasped a hand to her chest, as if the pressure of her palm could stop the irregular heart palpitations she'd been experiencing for the past six hours. Linda had been sick with an abscessed tooth for four days, and her doctor had warned that the advanced infection could pose a serious risk to her health. Around dinner time that evening, her heart had suddenly begun beating irregularly. Now, in the unmarked hours of the night, the palpitations were at their worst; her heart fluttered and flopped like a butterfly crushed in the paws of a cat.

She reached into her sweater pocket and fingered the slip of paper there. Should she call? Was it worth waking her doctor in the middle of the night? She didn't want to take a chance with something as serious as her heart. Then again, maybe she was being paranoid. Maybe it was nothing more than a reaction to stress. But what if it *wasn't* as simple as that? She didn't know what to do, and there was no one to help her make the decision.

She had never felt quite this alone. Ever.

Linda caught the neon glare of a beacon in the night: a twenty-four-hour supermarket. She turned into the lot and parked quickly. As she walked across the empty lot, two drunks staggered past the store entrance. Linda clutched her purse tighter and hurried inside.

The bright lights and familiar surroundings calmed her for the moment. The store was deserted, except for box boys stocking shelves for the next day's business. Looking for anything to keep her in the presence of other people—even if they were only anonymous clerks—Linda roamed the aisles for something to buy. In the cosmetic department, she tested all of the makeup samples and took the computerized skin analysis she'd never found the time for before.

By the time she exhausted that resource, she remembered a few items she needed at home. She paid for her purchases and, still clutching her purse tightly, walked cautiously back to the car.

All evening her mind had been repeating God's promise to his children: "I will never leave you nor forsake you." Yet there was no denying it; Linda felt both forsaken and alone.

Looking for a few good friends?

When Linda got home she went straight for her Bible. David had managed to find comfort by writing the Psalms; maybe she'd find a little by reading them.

In Psalm 46 she read:

God is our refuge and strength,
an ever-present help in trouble.
Therefore we will not fear.
The Lord Almighty is with us;
the God of Jacob is our fortress.
Be still, and know that I am God.
(verses 1-2, 7, 10, NIV)

Linda's heartbeat was still fluctuating—although not as wildly—as she turned out the light and crawled into bed. Lying in the dark, she thought about the fact that God doesn't expect us to have faith enough to *avoid* the anxious moments—just faith enough to rely on him *during* the anxious moments.

She also thought about the third parties. David, for example, was a third party. Linda would never meet him—on earth, anyway—but reading about his experiences had helped Linda feel a little less alone. She might feel lonely, but at least she wasn't the only one to know what *that* felt like.

Linda had a chance to consider third parties again the next day at work, when she told a Christian coworker about the midnight crisis.

"Why didn't you call me?" the other woman remarked. "I would have come over and sat with you."

Linda shook her head. "It was so late. I didn't want to wake anyone up in the middle of the night like that." But even as Linda answered, she caught a look in the woman's eye, and she realized her friend was entirely sincere. Maybe Linda *could* have called—*should* have called. Perhaps she had missed out on an opportunity for blessing, an opportunity to see God's promises fulfilled through the willing heart of yet another third party.

Face it: We need each other. There's nothing spiritual or even desirable about working through a crisis, just you and

God. Fellowship, networking, and vulnerability among believers are some of the most powerful methods God uses to minister to our needs.

And it goes right back to wholeness, doesn't it?

Linda and I believe that, for single mothers, married mothers, fathers, teens, and old folks, a big part of wholeness is knowing how to interact as complete persons with the people who love us . . . which means that spiritual facades and perfect images are out. Honesty and vulnerability are in.

When we ache, it's okay to let someone we love know that we're hurting. When we struggle with sin, we need to establish accountability with someone who knows about our struggle. When we're lonely, we can find compassion and companions if we're willing to take the risk to open our hearts.

There are a lot of reasons to surround ourselves with a network of friends with whom we can share mutual support and accountability. But for single-parent families, these friendships provide an extra service: They not only provide comfort for the adult in the family . . . they can also help relieve children of the role of confidant to lonely parents.

While transparency with our children is a gift to them and to ourselves as well, single parents can rely too heavily on children for the emotional support they're not getting from a spouse. When we interviewed Dr. Ralph Ricco, psychologist, he said that parents who use their children almost as therapists—as depositories for unrestricted thoughts and fears—set their kids up for a lot of fears themselves. While he agrees that parents should not portray two-dimensional images to their children, his concern is that adults be transparent at appropriate levels with the appropriate age group. Having an adult with whom to share can help parents find this balance.

The significance of the third-party principle cuts across marital status, age groups, sex, and station in life. God's promises are true. He never leaves us nor forsakes us. Often the path he takes to our side is through the presence of a loving friend.

We really *do* need each other.

To date or not to date—that is the question. (Unfortunately, your kids probably think *they're* the ones with the answer!)

Linda couldn't help but smile as she stacked the dinner dishes into the dishwasher. She had some news to share with her sons, and she was waiting for just the right moment.

As soon as the kitchen counter was clear, Linda reentered the living room and approached the couch where the boys sprawled. Chris was starting some homework and Dallas was reading a comic book.

"Hey guys, something, oh, interesting happened today." Linda giggled in spite of herself.

Chris stirred. "Yeah?"

"You'll probably get a big kick out of it like I did."

"What, Mom?" Dallas sighed. He wanted to return to the comic book.

"I got asked out on a date today by a very interesting gentleman." Linda chuckled, waiting for some sign of life from her boys. When nothing happened, she hurried to explain further. "For dinner. On Friday."

"You're *going?*" eleven-year-old Dallas gasped. "You're going on a *date?*"

Chris just stared at his mother with wounded eyes.

Suddenly Dallas burst into angry tears. He flung threats bitterly. He said he would run away, kill the guy, or sabotage the date. Then he exploded up from the couch, ran from the room, and slammed the bedroom door behind him.

Linda sat, stunned, in the silence after the bomb.

In the following days, Linda tried to get Dallas to talk about his feelings, to find out what fears or needs had fueled his rage that night. But Dallas had snapped tighter than a clam. He refused to answer any of Linda's questions and declined to offer any information on his own. As far as Dallas was concerned, the case was closed.

Maybe this wasn't going to be as easy as Linda had hoped . . .

Mothers learning to date the second time around rarely find it an easy transition. Suddenly a decision that used to be relatively personal becomes an issue for the entire family to wrestle with.

To make matters worse, sons and daughters helping to shape the experience for Mom are doing so with maturity levels appropriate to their ages. I mean, it's hard to ask a eleven-year-old to respond to his mother's need for companionship with the savvy of an adult. Kids are going to respond as kids.

I learned this firsthand when Dallas and I had a chance for a heart-to-heart one night at Linda's home. Linda had finally gotten past Dallas's communication blockade when she convinced him to grant me an interview for our book. She pointed out that his perspective—as the son of a dating single parent—could add a whole new dimension to our research. She finally offered to pay him a healthy sum for his time if he would agree to be interviewed. He agreed, and one week later—as Linda, Chris, and Kaitlyn prepared cornbread to accompany a pot of Dallas's homemade chili—Dallas and I met in the recreation room at Linda's apartment complex.

At one point in our interview, Dallas informed me that when he was old enough to date girls, his mom could date. *No* sooner than that.

Knowing that Dallas's mind was on our interview—but his stomach was with the pot of chili bubbling upstairs—I asked him to imagine something with me. "Pretend you're really hungry. Starving. Famished. And all you can think about is a big bowl of chili."

Dallas nodded, his mouth starting to water.

"Now imagine that I'm not hungry yet," I added. "And I tell you, 'When *I'm* ready to eat chili, *you* can eat chili. But no sooner than that.' In the meantime, you're miserable. You have a need *now*. Should your need wait until I develop a need of my own? What would you do in a case like this?"

Dallas didn't even hesitate. "I'd eat anyway."

I pursued the analogy. "But what if I got *really* ticked?"

"I'd do what I wanted to do."

"But what if I stormed and yelled and made threats and ran into my room, slamming doors and pounding walls?" I was hoping by now the scenario was starting to sound familiar to Dallas.

Dallas shrugged. "You'd get evicted."

"Maybe not. *You* didn't get evicted when you had a fit about your mom dating."

Dallas grinned. "*I'm* a kid."

He'd gotten my message, and I'd gotten his. He didn't *have* to act like an adult—he was eleven.

Of course, this doesn't mean it's appropriate to ask women to put their personal lives on hold for eighteen years until the kids have matured—or, according to Dallas, until they're infatuated with their own dates.

They say hindsight is 20/20, and at this point Linda has a pretty clear view of how she might have made the dating transition easier for her family. She suggests that single parents begin early to build a network of friends around their families—friends whose support can help fill the gap left after the loss of a dad. With their own emotional needs a little closer to being met, kids are not as likely to sabotage Mom's efforts to meet her own. Also, an early network of caring friends can help kids visualize their mother's need for fellowship with both women and men, laying the foundation for a healthy understanding of future dating relationships.

For Linda, the transition into dating came late, years after she had fled an abusive relationship. But it came dramatically, a sudden shift from a lifestyle dedicated to the boys and her job and little else. For Dallas, his mother's sudden leap—from years of self-sacrifice to a real date with a man—was too great. He told me he figured this meant his mom was on the verge of remarriage, and their lives would never be the same. She's not, of course. But if Dallas reasons things out like an eleven-year-old, can anyone really blame him?

Even though the support of adult friends can help meet children's needs *and* prepare them for any deeper relationships a parent might pursue, single parents may still be plagued with guilt. Dallas led into it well when he told me he didn't get angry about the hours his mother spent on her full-time job or free-lance projects: "She's doing *that* for the family," he told me. "But dating's just for *her,* and she's got two kids to take care of, and she never has enough time anyway, and now she's going to take *more* time and date."

His perspective isn't limited to kids. Somewhere, in the back of their minds, many single parents share the same concept about dating. In light of all the other elements necessary for survival, dating can seem, well, a little selfish.

But it's not. If finding balance as working women means approaching life as whole persons rather than out of a series of fragmented roles, then we've got to be willing to recognize and evaluate *all* of our needs. And the need to share companionship, affirmation, and even love with other adults is an integral part of the complex makeup of men and women. Unless they want to risk a festering infection of resentment or a critical case of burnout, single mothers *need* to take the time to incorporate friendships of all kinds into their lives.

This serves an obvious need for the single mom—yet it also serves a purpose for her children. In a single-parent home, children can miss out on the chance to observe adults engaging in the intricate dance called "relationship." When single parents give adult friendships an appropriate place in their personal and family life, they're giving kids an important opportunity to learn about the give and take, cost and pleasure, joy and responsibilities inherent in godly relationships.

I have a mouth as big as Jackie Gleason's, or, I bark but I don't bite.

Linda tells a story of returning home from work one evening after an usually stressful day to find Chris and Dallas lounging in front of the Nintendo. All around them was evidence that a major pig-out had taken place between the time they'd arrived home from school and the moment Linda unlocked the front door.

Linda clamped her jaws shut and managed, through clenched teeth, to deliver a monotone mandate: "PLEASE. CLEAN. THIS. UP."

When the boys ignored her gracious warning, she upped the volume a notch. Her third statement held the restrained energy of a nuclear blast.

Chris, finally stirring from the video game, made the tragic miscalculation of thinking his mom could be joked out of her foul mood. He began to taunt and tease, then launched a playful wrestling match. In the scuffle, Linda banged her shin against the edge of a wall. It was the last straw. Any self-control Linda had left was replaced by the brief but blinding pain. Holding her shin and glaring at her sons, she let them have it with all the lung power she could muster.

When the storm blew over, the boys were quick to clean their mess and volunteer help with dinner. Moments later, as Dallas headed out the front door to empty the trash, Linda spotted their neighbor Alice coming out of her apartment. There was concern on her face. Dallas had left the front door hanging open, and Linda could hear Alice whisper, "Dallas, are you all right?"

Dallas answered politely, "Sure. How are you?"

"I mean, are you *sure* you're all right?" Alice asked again, with a sideways glance toward Linda's apartment.

Linda cringed. Of course, Alice had heard the yelling. And Alice thought—what *did* Alice think? That Linda beat the boys? That the screaming prompted by a throbbing shin was, instead, an incident of verbal abuse?

Alice, her handsome husband, and well-mannered son painted a picture of the perfect, traditional family. Linda sighed when she realized what kind of impression *her* little family had made on these neighbors.

A few days later, Linda ran into Alice in the stairwell. Linda apologized for disrupting the peace and explained that, although she had a big mouth, she never hit or maimed. Later that week, Alice and her husband had a fight that the whole neighborhood got to hear. Linda learned to keep her voice down after that, but she also learned that even the perfect-looking families weren't all that different from hers.

Society is just now beginning to view single-parent families with a degree of acceptance. But it's still easy for single moms or dads to feel their families are seen as defective, incomplete, or, at best, different. The scrutiny can seem harsh as the world watches for a mistake, a dysfunction, an imperfection stemming from the fact that the single-parent family just doesn't seem, well, whole.

What's worse, sometimes the misperception can come from within your own ranks! In recent months, Linda's older son,

Chris, has moved out on his own, leaving Dallas, now four-teen, as the last of Linda's three children to still live at home. For years, Linda has managed to preserve the dinner hour as "family time," asking that everyone in the household meet and eat together each evening. Recently, however, Dallas's ac-tivities have threatened to encroach on the time-honored tra-dition. When Linda raised the issue one evening, she met with a revealing response from her youngest son.

"Family time?" Dallas asked. "But this isn't a family. It's just you and me."

Ouch.

Linda admits that fostering—and preserving—a sense of wholeness within a single-parent family can be tough. It's a skill that demands constant vigilance. After all, as individu-als within a family mature—and as the family unit undergoes transitions and changes—there are myriad opportunities for misperceptions to take root. "It's one thing," Linda says, "to do everything in your power to make sure that your own sense of personal and family wholeness stays intact. But you also have to address this issue, on an ongoing basis, with every member of your family."

One last thought about this perception of family "whole-ness." It's important to remember—for *all* of us to remem-ber—that seeking *wholeness* as a family is not made null and void by the fact that we have not attained *perfection* as a family. Imperfections abound wherever there is a human heartbeat. Single- *and* dual-parent families run the risk of dysfunction, of somehow sending grown children into the world ill-pre-pared for life in the fast lane.

Perfection, therefore, is unattainable.

Wholeness, however, is another story.

Wholeness doesn't require a certain number of family members. It doesn't even require a couple. After all, if whole-ness is something we can strive for as individual women—

seeking integrity in the way we perceive and express our-selves—wholeness is certainly attainable for *any* combina-tion of persons bound by the commitments and privileges of family life.

The special challenges of single parenthood are nothing to sneeze at. They include combating loneliness, making dating palatable to kids, and learning to feel like a "whole" family, not to mention the financial straits that many single-income families find themselves living with daily. And unfortunately, there aren't any pat or easy answers. Yet two approaches, each brimming with potential, have been mentioned in the pre-vious pages, and both deserve a second reference.

First, take the time to develop a network of caring friends. This network might include other single parents, or even caring couples you know from church or work. And remem-ber that the network idea provides two-way ministry—you have much to offer to other parents, single or married, and their families. There is a give and take, an ebb and flow, inherent in any relationship that goes beyond the acquain-tance level. In your friendships, be willing to give . . . and be willing to receive. And take the time to cultivate and nurture and enjoy the relationships in your life; they can become life-lines in the midst of what often feels like a battering storm.

Second, don't be afraid to pursue personal wholeness, even as you discover ways to view your family as whole, rather than broken. The way to personal—and corporate—whole-ness as outlined in this book is applicable to women regard-less of their marital status. Learning to deal with appropriate—and inappropriate—guilt; seeking help for dys-functional or compulsive patterns; and developing realistic expectations are just a few of the many approaches that can make a difference in your life, and in the lives of the mem-bers of your family.

10

Becoming a Team Player

You're Not Just a Working Woman.
You're Part of a Working Family.

No man is an island.
And no woman an "islandess."
The decisions we make for ourselves
are also decisions we make for our families.

The clock radio clicked on. An old hit by the Eagles blared into the bedroom. Ann groaned and pulled the pillow over her head.

The music muffled, she lay there, head covered, until Rick rolled over with a grunt. "Get your alarm," he said, his voice thick and deep with sleep.

Ann flung her pillow to the floor and grabbed the clock. She throttled it till her knuckles were white. Then she jabbed at the reset button and the room fell into silence.

"Heartache tonight. Heartache tonight. I'll give *you* a heartache tonight," she mumbled at the mute radio. "Boy, do I have a headache this morning."

"Hangover?" Rick attempted some early morning humor. His eyes were still closed.

Ann glowered at her husband's back. *"Right.* Try working till 4:00 A.M."

"Oh, I get it. It *is* a hangover."

"Huh?"

"But not from being an alcoholic. You're a *work*aholic."

"Oh, brother," Ann groaned. "No sleep *and* I have to put up with the Sunshine Comic, as well."

Ann showered, dressed, and put on her face. By the time she got around to her mascara, she was muttering the words that had been echoing in her brain for the past half hour.

I don't have to live this way.

I don't have to live this way.

All my colleagues might be crazy, but I don't have to go crazy with them.

Ann had been pondering the matter ever since that morning over waffles, when Rick lectured Brittney on making her own choices about something as profound as syrup. But Ann knew the principle meant something in her life, too.

Now, cotton-headed, puffy-faced, and bleary-eyed after only three hours' sleep, Ann was almost ready to cry uncle. She was almost ready to admit that it was crazy for her to sacrifice any*thing* and any*one* to keep up with workaholic colleagues at the office.

Ann managed to get through the day with numerous trips to the coffee machine. At half past four, Ann's intercom buzzed. The voice of her agency's director crackled and popped through the speaker. "Ann, when you get a minute, I'd like to see you in my office." Fifteen minutes later, Ann was sitting across from Stephen Glaswell, head honcho of the agency. He was smiling.

"I read your proposal on the Paradise Burger account," he said.

"Oh." Ann knitted her brow in thought. If she needed to defend the proposal she had spent all night writing, she just wished she could remember half of what she'd written. Anything she wrote after 2:30 A.M. sort of blurred together now in her mind.

Stephen Glaswell was still smiling. "You'll be happy to note that I'm suggesting we follow your directions entirely. I was especially impressed with the marketing angle on the new breakfast items; I like the imagery of the kids and the syrup."

"Really?"

"Excellent proposal, Ann. Really excellent. I'm going to pass your work by Denning and the others."

"*Really? The board?*"

"Keep up the good work. And thanks. That's all I needed to see you about."

Ann fairly flew back to her office, those four minutes with Glaswell doing more for her adrenalin level than six pots of coffee. Sitting at her desk, chest-high in folders and art-work and galleys, Ann was jazzed. Pumped. Stoked.

"I *can* do it all," she told herself. "I *can* compete with the workaholics. And I can succeed. All I have to do is give up a little sleep. How I handle my nocturnal life is *my* business. My family doesn't suffer. And I get everything accomplished. It can work. It can really work!"

Later that evening, Ann turned down the bedcovers with a deep longing. She was more than ready to close her grainy eyes and get some much-deserved sleep.

Rick walked into the bedroom just before Ann reached up and pulled the lamp chain, plunging the room into black-ness. There was a bump in the dark. Rick yelped in pain. Ann bolted straight up and yanked on the light. Rick stood dou-bled over the foot of the bed, holding his shin in pain.

"Rick! Honey! Are you okay?"

"Sheesh, Annie," Rick moaned. "Didn't you see me in here before you turned out the light?"

"No. No, I'm sorry. Does it still hurt?"

"What does it look like?" he groaned, still hunched. "Does this mean you're gonna mow the lawn for me this weekend?"

"No."

"Then there's no use milking it, is there?" he asked.

"I'm sorry. Really sorry. Is it better yet?"

He winced. "I guess the pain's subsiding. It's already gone from excruciating to merely agonizing. I think throbbing comes next." Rick hobbled to the bedside. The mattress creaked as he sat on the edge next to Ann. "Actually, I didn't know you were going to sleep so soon. I wanted to congratulate you."

Ann beamed. "No kidding? About the proposal?"

"Yep. I'm proud of you, Babe." He was still rubbing his shin.

"That means a lot." Ann reached for her husband's hand.

"Well, it's true. And I'm thrilled the proposal's done. I just hope it's the last of its kind."

"What's *that* supposed to mean?" Ann's voice took on a sharp edge.

"You know. Your all-nighter," he explained.

"No, I don't know."

"C'mon, Ann. You know what I mean."

"Frankly, I don't." She pulled her hand from his.

"Don't get huffy. I'm just saying that's the kinda stuff we did in college, *not* the kind of stuff that works well with a family. You've been a grump since you woke up this morning."

"Grump! *Grump!* I am not a grump." Ann heaved the words at him. "How I manage my sleep is my business. I can handle it. It doesn't affect you."

Rick stared at Ann for a full half-minute. "You're serious, aren't you?" he finally said. "You honestly believe that. You don't even see how you've been impatient with Brittney. And you've ignored me all evening; I might as well be invisible. You're too tired to help with dishes, give Brittney her bath, or even watch a movie together. And you don't think it's any of my business?"

Sullen, Ann stared straight ahead.

"Baby." Rick leaned toward his wife, into her line of sight. She looked away. He took her chin in his hand and turned her face toward his. "You're not in this alone. We're in this together. What you do, how you live your life, makes a big difference here at home, just as my decisions impact you. You don't live in a vacuum. We're individuals, sure, but we're a family, too. Now, I can't ask you not to ever work all night again. But I can ask you to recognize the costs." He paused, then added, "And I can ask you to weigh them with care."

It goes right back to wholeness:
Seeing the *whole* picture—the whole family—
not just the part played by one—
even if that one is me.

Every time I think I can isolate my family from all the little details, pressures, deadlines, stresses, and challenges related to my line of work, Kaitlyn reminds me of the truth.

Kaitlyn has her own briefcase, a pink plastic one she likes to compare to my burgundy leather one. Sometimes she plays house with her dolls. Other times she leaves them with a pretend grandmother so she can go to "meetings." And when anyone asks Kaitlyn what she wants to be when she grows up, she always says "a mom." One day my mother asked Kaitlyn what moms do. Kaitlyn's answer? "Oh, moms are around the house and they work on the computer."

As a way of grading my influence on her, I asked her if moms ever cook or ever clean house. She paused, thought awhile, and said, "No." Then she changed her answer to "Sometimes."

I wasn't exactly thrilled with my grade.

The fact is, we *can't* isolate our loved ones from being impacted by our work lives. If we're burned out, guilt-ridden, overworked, and exhausted, they feel the loss. Women—and men—have a responsibility to weigh the effects their lifestyles and work styles have on family life. Our decisions *must* reflect the fact that they are not decisions made for one, but decisions that impact entire households.

And that's good news and bad news, folks. The *bad* news is that when we make unhealthy, unbalanced decisions for ourselves, we're making the same decisions for our entire family.

- If we allow ourselves to live with relentless guilt—justified or unjustified—our family suffers.
- If we pursue our careers with an unbalanced drive, our family suffers.
- If we maintain unrealistic standards, exhausting ourselves over tasks at home and at the office, our family suffers.
- If we play the martyr—giving, giving, giving, giving—at the expense of our own personal needs, our family suffers.
- If we deny ourselves sufficient sleep, proper food, adequate exercise, or occasional moments of peace and quiet, our family suffers.
- If we devote every non-office moment to the kids, abandoning our marriage in the process, the whole family suffers, including the kids.
- If stress drives us to some destructive form of coping—smoking, drinking, compulsive eating or spending, anxious worrying, temper tantrums, withdrawal, etc.—we don't suffer alone. Loved ones suffer, too.

But here's the good news. We share the good things, too. Things like challenges, achievements, growth, lessons, skill expansion, resources, responsibilities. . . .

You get the idea.

Working moms help bring home the bacon. They might even help bring home the dad.

Thursday evening, Robyn pulled into the driveway with a carload of groceries just as Jason and the girls were climbing out of the station wagon. Rachel was clutching the doll she took to "show and tell." Ruthie carried her school books and lunch pail.

As Robyn stepped out of her car, Jason met her for a kiss. "Rachel's day care asked me to remind you about next Wednesday," he said.

"Next Wednesday?" Robyn asked, wrestling a bag of food out of the back seat.

"Yeah. Parents' night. Remember?" Jason asked.

"Oh, Jason! Wednesday's my OA meeting. Let me think a minute—"

"No problem. I'll go."

"To Overeaters Anonymous?"

"Hardly. To Parents' night. It'll be fun." Jason took the bag from Robyn's hands. "By the way, Kenman called. We're having lunch tomorrow."

Robyn stopped and stared at her husband. "Does he want your answer? About his new business?"

"Yep."

"Do you know what you're going to tell him? Do you want another job? It would mean your nights and weekends, too."

Jason shrugged. "I told Kenman it would probably be temporary. Until sales pick back up. It could be good for us, Robyn. You could quit work. I know that's what you want."

"I suppose," Robyn answered slowly. Financial woes had forced her into her job at the copy machine plant. For the past four months, she'd spoken longingly of the day when she could quit. Now she wasn't so sure. . . .

Ruthie pulled at her father's arm. "C'mon Daddy, you promised."

"Okay, Munchkin. First help Daddy carry in the groceries. Here's a featherweight bag for you. Hey, Robyn. Robyn?"

Robyn jumped, startled out of her thoughts. "Huh? What?"

"Call us when dinner's ready. I've got a date."

"A date?"

"With Ruthie. I promised we'd put the kite together before dinner."

"Oh? Sure. Hey, leave the groceries," Robyn offered. "I'll take them in."

Robyn watched her husband and older daughter head around the side of the house, toward the gate to the backyard. Rachel's short legs pumped as she tore after them, yelling for them to wait. Jason turned and stopped, scooping his four-year-old into his arms as she ran.

Robyn was going to have to do some serious thinking about this moonlighting thing.

Just last week on some late-night talk show, I saw comedian Paul Rodriguez talking about the emphasis on family within Hispanic communities.

"You know how it is," he said. "Grandmothers, cousins, uncles, and aunts—lots of generations. Everyone's close. And my dad. When I was a kid, my dad was always right there for us. I mean, *right there.*"

And then he quipped, "You know, there's something to be said for unemployment."

It drew a laugh. But he's got a point. Togetherness requires time.

A friend of mine had the exact opposite problem. Miles was *over*employed. He put in double shifts at the plastics factory where he worked so his wife could stay home full-time with the boys. Miles didn't get home till long after the kids were in bed, and he slept past the time they left the house for school. He saw his sons on weekends. Five days a week, wife Emily was a single mother.

A couple of months ago they moved to a bigger house in an outlying residential area where the housing is more affordable. Their house payment will stay the same, yet Emily and the boys will have more room. Miles is continuing his overtime routine, working the long hours to provide material comforts—and a full-time mom—for his family. And now he's commuting two hours every day to do it. He never used to see his kids. Now he rarely sees his wife.

There's something to be said for stay-at-home mothering. Quite frankly, there's *a lot* to be said for it, and Linda and I believe making that kind of an investment in a family can be worth almost any price. It's certainly worth sacrificing things like:

- a sleek new car
- a bigger house
- that cross-country vacation
- nights on the town
- the landscaping, new pool, or paint job for the house

But it's not worth the cost of a husband. And it's not worth the loss of a dad.

Mornings at Robyn's home feel like a circus. And Friday morning—just hours before Jason's business lunch with Kenman—was no exception. Especially when Ruthie's science project escaped from its cage. Luckily, Robyn found the chameleon panting in the kitchen sink, its skin camouflaged a crusty brown to blend well with last night's dishes.

Somewhere between sack lunches, instant oatmeal, spilled milk, and frozen orange juice, Robyn caught Jason's attention. "We've got to talk."

"Sure. When?"

"Now," Robyn announced.

"You're kidding!"

"It's now or never, Jason. I was awake half the night thinking about this."

"Okay, but we've got a whole six minutes if you still want me to drop Ruthie off at school."

"I'll take her. I'll call work and tell them I'll be a little late. Girls, you go watch "Sesame Street" a minute while Mom and Dad talk. What? No, you won't be late for school. Ruthie, don't make a face."

The kitchen door swung shut behind the girls.

Robyn faced her husband. "Jason, the past four months have been, well, a little hard on me."

"I know, Robyn, and that's why I intend to—"

"Wait. Just listen. I'm trying to tell you I don't want you to take Kenman's offer. I mean, it's your decision. But in the past four months, my working has meant you've had time to be a dad. I've never seen the girls responding to you like they've been doing lately. And you seem happier, too. Less stressed. More, well, *here* for us. Emotionally. And physically, too. The girls seem really happy with the child-care arrangements. And, despite my complaining, I'm doing okay, too. The job has forced me to take stock of myself. It got me to OA, remember? I feel stress sometimes, but your efforts with the kids and the house really help. And I feel good about what I'm doing. I feel good about me."

"Robyn, are you sure—"

"Look. If I could quit work and still have you home in the evenings and weekends, I would do it. I'd quit tomorrow, and the girls could have a full-time mom and a part-time dad. But I think two part-time parents work better for this family than no dad at all. I remember what it was like for you before I started work. You were a stranger in your own house. And I'm just not willing to go back to that."

A long silence fell on the little kitchen, and on the man and woman sitting at the breakfast table. Jason reached over and picked up Rachel's Tommy Tippy cup, the one with the missing lid. He studied it for several minutes, turning it over and over in his hands. A drop of juice fell to the table, but Jason didn't seem to notice.

When he finally spoke, there was a tightness to his voice—as if his words were squeezing past a lump in his throat.

"You know," he said, still staring at the cup, "you're a pretty sharp woman." He cleared his throat and stood to leave, then paused at the threshold of the kitchen door to blow Robyn a kiss on one finger. She thought—although she couldn't tell for sure—that she caught the glimmer of a tear.

Take action first and ask questions later?
That works in the movies.
But try it at home and you're liable to lose
your viewing audience.
The family that decides together
works together.

For Robyn and Jason, being a working family means being a *whole* family.

For other families, becoming a whole family means improving communication and learning to make joint decisions.

When two more friends asked Jenny if she could watch their preschoolers during the day, Jenny said she'd let them know by Monday. If she said yes, it would increase the number of her lively charges to six. It might even mean purchasing some extra equipment, like booster chairs or nap pads. Yet it would mean added dollars to their skimpy budget. It was worth considering.

Saturday morning, over French toast, she discussed the idea with Jeff.

"It's your decision," Jeff responded between bites. "You spend every day with the kids. You need to decide how many you can handle."

Jenny shook her head. "It's broader than that, Jeff. I can't just leap into a decision. There are some things we've got to think about. Things like what the house can handle. Are your weekends going to be spent repainting walls and repairing fixtures? And if I've got six kids, you can bet I won't get the laundry done during the day like I have been. Can I fit it in my schedule at night? If not, can you fit it in yours? And what about Mathew? Can *he* handle the added little people? It's his turf, his toys, his space, you know. He's only a year old. What are *his* limits?"

"I wish we could ask him," Jeff admitted.

"I think that would be a good family policy to start practicing."

"Jenny, he can't even talk."

Jenny laughed. "Not *now*. I mean, as he's growing up. What a neat idea to include him on decisions that affect him!"

Melita feels the same way. She says familywide communication is the key to smooth sailing. Well, maybe not smooth sailing, but at least the avoidance of violent mutiny.

We met for lunch last week, and she spoke frankly about several decisions she is in the process of making.

"I've come to the realization that, as long as I live in southern California, I'll never buy a home. Not on one income, that is," she explained over a cobb salad with low-cal dressing.

"And that's important?" I asked.

Melita nodded. "Yes. I don't want Brenda growing up in an apartment all her life. I want her to have some space. And I can't ignore the fact that it would be wonderful to get out from under the feeling that we're barely making it financially. It would mean less stress for me, and more emotional space for Brenda. So, I'm toying with the idea."

"Where would you go?"

She brushed a raven lock behind her ear and shrugged. "There are banks in every city. And almost any city in the nation is more affordable than southern California. A decent three-bedroom house in most other states is less than half of what I'd pay here."

"Does Brenda know?"

"Oh, sure. I figured, years ago, that the best way to survive parenthood—especially single parenthood—was through really solid communication. She knows the final decision is up to me, but I keep her informed and ask for her input all along the way."

I looked at my friend with newfound admiration. "Well, it seems to be working."

Melita laughed. "Oh, it works great. Until she disagrees with me, that is. Then I usually kick myself and ask what I've gotten myself into!"

Working women can't do it alone. Our families have got to support us in our efforts, and we've got to support them with our decisions.

Good communication—and even joint decisions—are critical to the whole process. Remember, you heard it right here first—informed, consulted families are happy, healthy, *and cooperative* families.

I'm going to be honest (only because my husband will be reading this book and he knows the dirt): This is a tough concept for me to grasp.

My line of work isn't always easy for my family to live with. It's sporadic, project by project, deadline by deadline. That means it's hard to lock into a structured, daily schedule.

When I'm facing a deadline, my idea of a home-cooked meal is anything that requires more than two boxes or cans. And my idea of clean laundry? Any item of clothing that doesn't stand up or move on its own.

Larry helps. He helps a lot. In fact, his help is integral to my success as a working mom. And I can live with that. What I have a hard time with is the fact that Larry likes to be consulted as I make decisions to take on new projects. For some reason I'm still struggling to fully understand, he wants to help make the decision that will draft him into extensive housework and child care for impressive periods of time.

I guess that's why I know these last pages are important—not because I've got the problem licked, but because I know exactly where the pitfalls are (and am intimately acquainted with the bottom of every one of them).

There's no way around it (and believe me, I've tried). Part of developing wholeness as a family is communicating—and even brainstorming—as a family.

Once appropriate interchange and mutual decision-making have been fostered among members of a nuclear family, then the environment and relationships therein may be considered to be adequately prepared for introduction of another vital element of the working family: chores.

It's a six-letter, one-syllable word. And there's no easy way to say it. Yet, as working women, we've got to learn how to say it to our families, and say it in conjunction with two other little words: "Here's yours. . . ."

As a single parent, Linda has mastered the art of delegating chores to Dallas and—before they struck out on their own—Chris and daughter, Tami. For Linda, it hasn't been a matter of choice; it's been a matter of survival.

Linda has formulated five factors that can help turn the process into a success rather than a civil war:

- **Invite input up front.** Businesses that allow employees to own a piece of the company experience higher productivity and morale among their staffs. It makes sense; people are going to invest more energy where they have ownership. And the fastest way to help your family *feel* ownership in family matters is to let them *have* ownership. Encourage participation, not just at the manual labor stage, but from initial decisions on down the line.

- **Delegate according to strengths.** We can set our families up for failure—and ourselves up for constant battles—if we don't adhere to this principle. A son who loves organization and structure may be a better choice for setting the dinner table than an unstructured, outdoorsy daughter who shrivels at the thought of trying to remember on which side of the plate the knife goes. Let *her* mow the lawn instead.

Kaitlyn loves to run the canister vacuum, but she's good for about five minutes before she wears out. With a bottle of Windex and a paper towel, however, she can stay busy for at least fifteen minutes. Her sense of achievement gets a boost, and I get clean windows!

Appeal to a daughter's artistic flair by asking her to wrap all the Christmas presents this year. Encourage a son's interest in cooking by asking him to prepare an entire meal each week. If you have a husband who meets the public every day and comes home overstimulated and frazzled, don't ask him to do the grocery shopping, where he'll clash carts with strangers and jockey for position in the cashier's line. Instead, delegate a responsibility that feeds his need for solitude and quiet. Washing and folding clothes, for example, is time consuming, yet doesn't demand interaction with anything living.

■ **Give authority with responsibility**. Exercises in mere order-taking belong in the military. In the civilian world, men, women, and children perform better when they have an appropriate level of control delegated with the task. When Larry washes the dishes, he makes a night of it. He sets up a portable TV or dons Walkman headphones, and he's at the sink for hours. I may have a faster system, but I've got to be willing to let him do *his* job *his* way. If I'm not, I'll very likely find myself resuming the authority *and* the responsibility for the dishes that night.

- **Create accountability.** Responsibility plus authority *does not* relieve a single one of us of accountability. Accountability can be achieved any number of ways, including the always faithful star chart, privileges granted and withheld, and simply letting loved ones experience the natural ramifications of a dropped responsibility.

- **Make adjustments**. No one wants to feel that he or she has been drafted into any responsibility for life. The following approaches can help break the monotony: rotating chores, relieving chores during school finals, upgrading authority with increased maturity, or delegating chores in conjunction with a course at school (for example, delegate a meal each week while your son or daughter is in a cooking class in school; find chores that will complement the skills your son develops as he earns Boy Scout badges). Is your husband working shorter hours one week due to a hold-up on a project at work? Readjust—or decrease—the family's chores that week so everyone can spend more time with Dad. Are kids home for summer vacation? It's another opportunity to reevaluate the workload. Every month or so, call a family meeting to invite input, reevaluate the workload, make necessary adjustments, and praise everyone for pulling their share!

- **Use positive reinforcement**. Making a hullabaloo each time a kid makes the bed implies that he or she is going beyond the call of duty. Keep the fireworks in the garage, or your family may conclude they're doing you favors instead of contributing to a team effort.

Having addressed that extreme, let us add that heartfelt expressions of appreciation are *crucial* to your family's success as a working team.

Delegating doesn't save time or energy all the time. Mothers of young children, especially, may find it easier to do a job themselves rather than delegate. Single parents, in particular, can feel guilty about delegating chores that cross stereotypical gender roles.

Yet delegating enables working women to juggle their many responsibilities with success. It prepares daughters and sons for their very likely futures as working women and husbands of working wives. Finally, it can create a team spirit between spouses. Holding down a full-time job often gives women a better appreciation for their husbands' labor; likewise, pulling an appropriate share of the work at home can help husbands gain a deeper understanding of the many demands on their wives' time, as well as the skill with which those demands are met.

For women who *still* find themselves confronting balking husbands who'd rather take two aspirin than take out the trash, consider this (and then show it to your husband):

Shirley Sloan Fader, author and columnist for *Ladies' Home Journal*, lists four areas in which men will suffer if their wives, overcome by the demands of household and career, return to full-time homemaking:

- ■ If women exit the workplace, men will reclaim the responsibilities of sole breadwinner. For a family that has grown accustomed to the higher living standard that Mom's paycheck allowed, the task for Dad will be formidable.

- Twenty years ago, the idea of men changing careers in mid-life was virtually unheard of. Today, husbands of working wives are finding it economically possible to change jobs, accept more interesting work for less pay, or go into business for themselves—options that, without a second income, could be irresponsible or even disastrous.

- When a husband loses a job, the income of a working wife can be the factor that saves him from accepting just any job at any wage. A new pattern is emerging, according to Brenda Ruello, a partner in an international executive-search firm, and that is "the luxury of search time to locate the best job opportunity."

- Finally, men whose wives contribute financially are enjoying a better quality of life with regard to their relationships. They are finding the economic freedom to say no to overtime, heavy travel, and unattractive job responsibilities that might have been financial necessities without that second income. Many are discovering the joys of parenthood in a way their fathers never had the chance to do.

Shirley Sloan Fader concludes with these words: "Only by more equitable sharing of the family's domestic, as well as its economic, responsibilities can both wife and husband win. If she can't have it all, he quickly will discover that neither can he."[1]

Notes
1. Shirley Sloan Fader, "Men Lose Freedom If Women Lose Ground," *Ladies' Home Journal* (February 2, 1987).

CREATIVE PROBLEM SOLVING

You want to learn to drive the car?
This is lesson #1.

11

Creative Problem Solving

Finding Solutions That Work

You say you don't know where to start?
Look on the bright side:
If you've got problems,
you've got plenty of places to begin.

The bad news is that I really need to improve my skills at creative problem solving. The good news is that I've got plenty of raw material to work with.

There's no shortage of problems. Especially for working women. And particularly for working moms. After all, part of the definition of *mother* is someone who vicariously experiences every crisis of every member on the family roster.

Something happened early on in my experience as a mother that showed me to what extent I apply that definition in my own life. Three weeks before her third birthday, Kaitlyn came home from preschool and announced she had a "boyfriend." Actually, he was an older man—someone in the four-year-olds' class.

Two days later my daughter came home in tears. Right there, right at "their" spot in the sandbox, Frankie had told her he didn't want to be her boyfriend anymore. There was (sob) another woman.

Kaitlyn took it hard.

I took it even harder.

I realized just how hard I was taking it the next day as I faced the cashier at Target and handed her sixty dollars for a stack of high-fashion toddler clothes. I guess I figured that, while I couldn't help Frankie make the right dating decisions, I sure could help him regret making the wrong one.

However, before I could teach Kaitlyn to say "Frankie, eat your heart out" with just the right flair, she came home from preschool with good news. She and Frankie were together again.

When I asked about the other girl, Kaitlyn beamed. "She's his girlfriend, too! We're *both* his girlfriends!"

Quite a boy, that Frankie.

I started to explain the concept of two-timing, but decided against it. My daughter was growing up too fast already. I wanted to leave something for the kindergarten years.

We made it through that crisis. And we've made it through others since. Still, I have to wonder how I'm going to make it through the next twenty years. After all, I barely made it through my own dating years. Now I've got to survive Kaitlyn's, too?

The real clincher is that I'm not sure which heartaches are harder to experience—mine or hers.

Problems are like Mondays; good solutions are like Saturdays. You *know* they go hand in hand, but you *feel* like you're being shortchanged.

Problems are abundant.

Good solutions are as longed for as a three-day weekend—and seem just about as rare.

Yet the real fact of the matter is that every problem has a solution. Most problems have more than one. The key lies in recognizing them.

Linda read somewhere that if you can think of only two solutions to a problem, neither of those solutions is the right one.

In this book Linda and I talk a lot about wholeness. For a lot of us working women, that means taking our focus off our roles and expanding it to include all aspects of our personhood.

Creative problem solving isn't so different. The first step involves taking our focus off our problem and expanding it until *every* area of our lives becomes a potential setting for the discovery of a solution. When on the prowl for a creative solution, the key principle is this: No nook or cranny is off-limits. The little sucker could be hiding anywhere.

I bet you'd never guess that the solution to a painful leg rash might be found in a nail clipper. Or that the answer to successful potty training might be waiting in the freezer.

Several years ago, my mom developed, as a reaction to stress, a serious rash on the calves of both legs. Her nervous, constant scratching—prompted by the stress as well as the incessant itching—kept the rash from healing. She consulted doctors, books, and pharmacists. She tried ointments, balms, and dressings. The solution seemed out of reach. In reality, it was at her very fingertips all along.

One day, in sheer desperation, my mom cut off all her nails—down to the nubs. She couldn't scratch if her life depended on it. The first day was pretty uncomfortable. By the second day, the rash was less inflamed. Within the month— her faithful nail clippers always in reach—my mom's rash faded into history.

But perhaps my favorite example of creative problem solving comes from Christine, who got it from Dr. Dobson.

Christine's son Paulie was in the throes of potty training. And, to be honest, he wasn't real keen on the idea of urinating in the same bowl of water he uses to bathe Theodore, the stuffed turtle, when Mom isn't looking.

Christine knew Paulie was fairly accident-proofed as long as he was ushered into the bathroom three to four times a day. But Paulie rarely wanted to cooperate. He simply refused to produce the goods. Toilet time became a battleground. Fortunately for Christine, that's when she discovered the letter. It was written by another distraught mom and published in James Dobson's *Focus on the Family* magazine.

Dr. Dobson's solution wasn't complicated. It didn't use food as a bribe. It didn't require begging or groveling on the part of mothers who would almost give up their firstborn rather than find another pee-puddle on the carpet. And, unlike the expensive bells-and-whistles girdle that startles kids out of a year's growth everytime they wet, Dr. Dobson's solution didn't cost a dime.

He simply suggested freezing colored water into rainbow ice cubes and dropping a few ice cubes into the toilet bowl at potty time, along with instructions to take aim and shoot.

Suddenly potty training wasn't such a chore. In fact, it was almost more fun than going to the arcade.

Now *that's* the genius of a man who knows how to solve problems with flair.

Creative problem solving reaps big rewards. If you don't believe me, just ask the Grand Poobah of Joy.

My husband is dean of the College of Business at Dallas Baptist University. In his career in higher education, he's enjoyed numerous opportunities to address students and even faculty about the subject of creative problem solving. During his classes or seminars on the topic, Larry always tells the story of Ben and Jerry's gourmet ice cream in Waterbury, Vermont.

The company was founded in 1978 by—who else?—Ben and Jerry. At that time, Ben Cohen and Jerry Greenfield, both twenty-four years old, had a problem. The bagel business they'd talked about starting required forty thousand dollars for the bagel machine alone—nearly four times the amount they'd scraped together via savings, Jerry's father, and the bank. Their creative solution, however, was to shift gears. They enrolled in a five-dollar ice-cream-making correspondence course, converted an abandoned gas station into an ice cream parlor, and began making deliveries from the back of a VW Bug.

In the early 1980s, as their homegrown business sprouted like a weed, Ben and Jerry faced another dilemma: the acquisition of more than one hundred employees and a large factory facility had increased production but decreased the "family feel" of the business. Their creative solution was to appoint Jerry as the official Grand Poobah of Joy. Jerry looked for ways to boost morale in the growing company. He installed a top-of-the-line stereo system along the factory line, initiated a two-quart ice cream allowance per employee per week, and offered a one-dollar reward for catching a pit in the supposedly pitted cherries before a stone had a chance to jam the machinery.

Sometime later, the company launched a full Committee of Joy, and the events and parties dreamed up by the committee have become the stuff of legends. There was Barry Manilow Day, held on the musician's birthday, during which loudspeakers played Manilow songs and employees wore Barry Manilow buttons and ate Barry Manilow birthday cake. There was also Deface the President Day, during which a caricature of company president Fred Chico Lager was enlarged and reproduced, giving all three hundred employees a chance to compete at doodling, coloring, scribbling, or otherwise embellishing the features of their fearless leader. There have been Halloween dress-up days and Thanksgiving turkey raffles. Santa Claus even visited the plant one week before Christmas, telling reindeer stories and acquiring wish lists from good employees.

In 1982, a new problem demanded a solution. Ben and Jerry had become disillusioned with the fact that their business—despite their many efforts—had managed to become, well, a real business. They wanted to do something they described as "more significant," feeling they had become nothing more than a "mindless cog in the overall economy, taking in money with one hand and paying it out with the other, adding nothing." The creative solution was to make the company a force for social change. They founded Ben & Jerry's Foundation, which receives 7.5 percent of the company's pre-tax dollars, distributing it via a variety of social causes and agencies.

In 1985 the company faced yet another crisis as competitors Pillsbury and Kraft, makers of Häagen-Daas and Früsen Gladje premium ice creams, tried strong-arm tactics to keep Ben & Jerry's ice cream out of the Boston area. Ben and Jerry's creative solution? They mounted a "What's the Dough-Boy Afraid Of?" advertising campaign that drew national attention and sparked the power of public opinion.

Today, Ben & Jerry's ranks third in the nation's premium ice-cream market. The latest problem? In the words of cofounder Ben Cohen, "Our only fear is that we'll go more mainstream, less weird, and less socially responsible."

Knowing their penchant for creative solutions, my guess is that they'll find a way around that roadblock.

The dos and don'ts of creative problem solving.

We interviewed Dr. Larry Linamen (sounds official, doesn't it?) regarding the process of solving problems with a creative flair. He pointed out that, too often, men and women aren't creative thinkers because we've been conditioned not to exceed status quo.

Larry retold the familiar story of the woman who, every Sunday as she prepared the family dinner, sliced off the end of the roast before popping it in the oven. One day a friend asked about the strange custom. The woman admitted she didn't know the reason, but that she had learned it from her mother. The question sparked her curiosity, and that week she asked her mother about the custom. Mom said she'd picked it up from *her* mother. A few weeks later, the woman visited her grandmother and asked the matriarch about the strange custom. The old woman cackled. She said that, back on the farm, she'd had only one small pot and that she had to slice the ends off the roast so the hunk of meat wouldn't hang over the sides of the pot.

"Too often we go through life just doing whatever people tell us," Larry added. "We don't ask questions; we don't come to conclusions ourselves; we may not even understand why we've been told to approach a problem in a limiting manner."

He attributes part of the problem to educational systems that don't encourage creativity. "Too often young people receive greater awards for conformist thinking than for coming up with anything new or innovative. Something off-track in a term paper or art project is penalized. The person who comes up with a wild plan is considered to be rowing through life with one oar out of the water. In our MBA programs, we turn out people who can crank out numbers, get the bottom line, calculate all the ratios. But just because we can come up with numbers doesn't mean we know how to solve the problem."

But there is hope. It begins by knowing—and practicing— the following steps to personal creativity:

- Identify your creative period. Some people think clearly in the morning hours, when the day is new. Others can't see straight until after eleven in the morning or their sixth cup of coffee, whichever comes last. Still others come alive just about the time David Letterman is signing off the air.

- Allow a block of time *every* day for creative thinking, preferably during your creative period. According to Larry, no less than a twenty-minute block of time will do. Less than that and your brain doesn't have enough time to clear away the cobwebs and anxieties and make room for creative thoughts. Finding a half-hour block of time—especially for a working mother—seems like a formidable task. But this small investment of time, consistently made, will reap major returns in hours and energy saved.

- Curiosity frequently implies creative ideas. Forget what you've been told all your life about curiosity being the number-one cause of death among felines. Encourage your curiosity—it's often the impetus for creative solutions.

- Use the personal analogy method whenever possible. Imagine yourself as an inanimate object if it relates to a problem you're trying to solve. Men and women, imagining they were traffic lights swaying in a gusty wind, helped develop the guide wires that today keep traffic lights from doing that very thing. Men and women—pretending to be expensive fur coats trying to guard themselves against shoplifting—came up with the idea of security chains that keep the coats linked to the display.

■ Maintain an idea notebook. Write down that sudden flash of insight you have while standing in line at the bank or in the shower at home. Write down the creative ideas or solutions of other people. Write down all the little nagging problems that demand a creative solution. Then, when you sit down for your half-hour creative thinking session in the morning, you won't waste time trying to remember exactly what it was you needed to solve.

■ Borrow creative ideas. There's no need to reinvent the wheel. If something worked for a friend or someone you read about in a magazine, adopt, adjust, and enjoy!

■ Finally, one of the most important principles, according to Larry, is to consider every source when you're looking for an answer. Don't be afraid to try the unconventional or to approach the problem from an unusual perspective.

One creative solution can make a lot of difference in your world.

Robyn knew she needed a creative solution as soon as she and Jason decided she would continue working. Now that her job wasn't a temporary measure, she knew something had to change. She was tired of being underestimated simply because she was a woman. She was tired of being overlooked for responsible assignments, being made to feel that she was second-class, while men at her same level got all the respect.

She realized that demanding respect from her boss wouldn't be effective. Changing jobs wasn't an option she cherished, yet neither was being patronized daily.

She began looking for creative ways to communicate that she didn't fit the stereotype with which she'd been pegged.

Her first action was to look and act the part she *wanted* to play in the office. She upgraded her office wardrobe as well as her professionalism on the job. She still remembers how conspicuous she felt the first day she took a briefcase to work. "For three days I carried this empty briefcase to and from the office," she told me over the phone. "I felt pretty stupid and was sure someone would catch a glimpse inside and then I'd be fully humiliated. On the fourth day I stuck a newspaper and some files inside."

She began typing memos instead of scribbling them on a memo scratch pad. She began answering her extension using her first *and* last name. When she noticed that the office leaders always left the building for lunch instead of gossiping at their desks over brown bags, she began leaving the office, too, even though some days she just ate lunch in her car.

Mr. Bookman continued asking her to make the coffee and straighten the kitchen, so Robyn began going to work ten minutes early—before anyone else arrived—to get the coffee started. Facing a full coffeepot every morning, Robyn's boss didn't have to think about who should make the coffee. It was no longer a topic of conversation between Mr. Bookman and Robyn—and it no longer served as a daily reinforcement of Mr. Bookman's homemaker image of Robyn. A couple of weeks later, once the coffee issue was far from the forefront of her boss's mind, and as Robyn's more professional image began to take shape in coworkers' minds, Robyn approached the two other administrative assistants—both men—in her office. She enlisted their help in handling morning coffee duties on a weekly basis.

Two months later, one of the company's account representatives left to work for a competitor, and Mr. Bookman asked Robyn to advertise the available position in the paper. Instead, she approached him for the job, pointing out that training a new administrative assistant would cost the company much less than training a newly hired salesperson. She pointed out that her familiarity with the company would enable her to make the transition quickly into the new responsibilities. Mr. Bookman scratched his head, scribbled some numbers on a memo pad, wrinkled his forehead, and cleared his throat. Then he shook Robyn's hand. She had the job.

Creative problem solving: For one to seven players.

Robyn found a creative solution for her problem, but the process isn't limited to individuals. Entire office staffs or families can play the game. It's called *brainstorming*.

When we interviewed my husband, he gave a second list of dos and don'ts for the group version of the game. For a successful brainstorming session at your home or office:

- Aim at involving three to seven people. Less than that and you lose the synergism generated by a group. More than that and it becomes intimidating to speak up.

- Everyone joins in spontaneously—no permission is needed to speak.

- No criticism allowed. When brainstorming, there are no "bad" ideas. Even the wildest pitch may hold the seeds of a workable solution.

- Freewheeling is encouraged. There are no rules, no parameters. If your group thinks better while playing Nerf basketball, set up the net. Your brainstorming goal is to come up with solutions, not to follow Robert's Rules of Order.

- The quantity and variety of solutions are directly related to the quality. If your group comes up with five similar solutions, you've barely touched the tip of the iceberg. However, if you come up with thirty solutions ranging from hiring a clown to painting the Empire State Building, you have much better odds of hitting on "the right one."

- Combinations and improvements are encouraged. Piggyback ideas one onto the other: "If we took that same apple but peeled it instead . . . "

- Take notes during the session.

Use these guidelines the next time your family brainstorms over chores or finances, or the next time you pull together a coalition of moms in your company to brainstorm over child-care solutions, or whenever you find yourself on a task force to reduce spending in your department by 90 percent, or some similar miracle.

At home or at the office, you *can* create an environment that encourages the long-lost art of creative thinking.

Linda and I believe that *nothing* provides opportunities for creative problem solving quite like the formidable task and privilege of making a home *and* making a living. What many women are trying to do today has never been done before. We're pioneers. Few of us had mothers and grandmothers as role models for the unique balancing act we're attempting. We *have* to be creative because traditional solutions may not work for the challenges we face.

You'll find five of these challenges—deciding to stay home with young children, fending off the lure of an office romance, attaining and maintaining power in the workplace, calling a truce between women employed and women at home, and preparing our kids for the choices of tomorrow— discussed in the following chapters. And you'll encounter creative solutions for each of the five.

Tackling life's dilemmas with a creative flair takes conscious effort. Like any valuable skill, it takes time to learn. But it's worth the investment. And it's worth the risk.

While working together on this book, Linda told me a poignant story about a single moment that changed her perspective about taking the kinds of risks that creative thinking requires. It was the moment that inspired Linda to eventually follow through with a rather drastic solution she'd been pondering for months: moving her family across the nation, to a new start and better life in the more-affordable Midwest.

A desolate, brush-strewn hill rises behind the southern California apartment complex that Linda and her boys at one time called home. It's the perfect kind of hill for hiking off excess energy with rambunctious kids. It's also a haven of solitude when the stresses of daily living begin to feel like a pounding twenty-drum band.

One day, fed up to *here* with the struggles of single parenting, Linda pulled on her Nikes, grabbed a jacket to ward off the fall chill, and headed for the hill. She was tired of striving, tired of the constant effort her life seemed to require. True, she'd thought of a few creative solutions—like moving out of California to another part of the country where the pace is slower and an average home doesn't cost a quarter-million dollars. But all the really creative options seemed risky. They held potential, but they didn't seem as secure as her current path, even though *that* felt like the Indy 500 most of the time.

Linda walked the dirt paths crisscrossing the hill, kicked stones, and stood, neck arched, staring at wisps of clouds trailing the sky.

Suddenly a bird cut against the wind, a silhouette against the blue. Dropping near the ground, the tiny creature beat the air with her wings, striving for speed. Linda watched the bird, seeing something of herself in its frantic labor.

Then the bird arched and rose, pumping harder, faster, higher into the sky. The ground fell away behind the tiny, beating wings. The security of trees and nests and food dropped farther away, until they were mere specks in the distance.

And then something happened.

As she reached the heights, the bird gave one last shove with tired wings, then spread her feathers and soared.

That's what the right solution—a creative solution—can do for us.

12

To Work or Not to Work?

*Taking a Second Look at What's Best for
You and Your Family*

"The next decade will bring a trend toward homecoming.
Women will leave work to go home, open small businesses,
and have babies."[1]

It's happening all across America. Waitresses, bank presidents, secretaries, factory workers, lawyers, and even TV anchorwomen are taking second looks at hectic lives and making tough decisions about the way they spend their days. Many are quitting work altogether. Others are dropping to half-time or just a day or two each week.

Taking the plunge and deciding to "go home" is scary.

There are financial matters to consider, and matters of identity.

Personal fulfillment is an issue. So is career advancement.

One article Linda and I read even suggested that working women who leave full-time jobs to return to the home front should consider that they're undoing the hard-earned gains of a generation of feminists: "Instead of moving forward to fill these hard-won management-level positions, the women of this generation [are retreating]—of their own free will—

into the cocoons of domesticity from which their mothers came.... The toll will be enormous."[2]

Yet the women who are doing it are applauding the results. Here's what some of them are saying:

- "The pay isn't great, long hours, lots of worries, but the fringe benefit is asleep in the next room."[3]

- "Before I had a baby, I always dreamed of making a valuable contribution to the world. When my child was a baby I knew that this was it. I would never be as important to someone as I was right then. You are the center of that child's universe."[4]

- "It was painful to give up my job. My work as a clinical social worker was a major part of my life. My identity was totally wrapped up in it. I started having professional guilt and mother guilt, and it got harder and harder to move between the two roles. But then, somehow, it all became clear: Maureen was my priority. Now that I'm home? I wouldn't go back for a million bucks. I'm having so much fun."[5]

- "Shortly after I had two children very close in age, we hired a live-in and I went to work. But the cost was too great to the kids. They weren't happy, weren't emotionally secure. It became obvious in their behavior. When kids aren't secure, they misbehave more, which causes more stress in the home. When I decided to quit working, they became well-adjusted children again. For my family? Work caused more problems than it solved."[6]

■ "I'd been in market research for eleven years when I decided to cut back to a part-time schedule to be with my one-year-old daughter. It wasn't a decision I made lightly; I worried about it for months. But I have my whole life to do market research. My daughter is little only once."[7]

Taking the plunge from two incomes to one? You've got to consider the bottom line . . . And whether it's scrawled in red ink or in black.

In one survey, eight out of ten working women agreed with the statement: "If I could afford it, I would rather be home with my children."[8] In another survey, nine out of ten women agreed with the statement that most women work full-time because they need the money.[9]

A lot of women—including single parents and women whose husbands are unemployed or earn little—*do* need the money. These women, and others, may not have much of a choice.

But a surprising number of women have more choices than they realize. If you're one of the many women who wishes she could spend more time at home but is convinced her budget wouldn't survive the cut, think again.

Here are three questions you can ask yourself to help you identify your family's bottom line:

1. What am I really earning after child care, dinners out, convenience food from my grocer's freezer, career wardrobe, dry cleaning bills, etc.?

Many women find, when it's all said and done, that they're working for two or three dollars an hour, hardly enough to compensate for the stress and exhaustion generated by working.

2. What are my hard-earned dollars going toward? And is it worth it?

A report in *The Family in America* states that the earnings of working wives are as likely to pay for fast food and paper plates as for a piano or stove. The report concludes: "This new study may come as good news to the nation's delicatessens. But what does it mean when higher household income leaves behind nothing permanent except day-care receipts and a mound of empty hamburger wrappers?"[10]

The *Wall Street Journal* reports: "Two-earner families spend significantly more on food away from home, child care, women's apparel, gas and motor oil, according to the government's Consumer Expenditure Survey. Families with full-time working wives also spend much more than one-earner families on mortgage or rental costs." [11]

Even when our incomes result in tangible purchases, are they really things we couldn't live without? A woman responding to a *Redbook* survey wrote: "The majority of women in my neighborhood claim they couldn't survive financially unless they worked. And that's true—if they are to pay for their two new cars, big-screen TV, VCR, new home, plush furnishings . . . "[12]

3. At what expense am I purchasing these items? What are they costing in terms of stress, the development of my children, the atmosphere of my home, and the quality of my life?

Author Deborah Fallows, interviewed in *People* magazine, says, "Parents are the most important people in their children's lives. Yet very often the children barely see them."[13] She quit a full-time job as assistant dean at Georgetown University to become a full-time mother, an occupation, according to *People*, that most of her peers equated with brain death. But for Deborah it was the right choice.

Regarding her plunge into full-time mothering, Deborah adds: "If quality time were all that mattered there would be no difference, say, between a couple that dated regularly and one with the experience of actually trying to live together under the same roof. Nonquality time might not sound very exciting, but mine with Tommy and Tad has been rewarding for all of us. It has consisted of hours in the park, afternoons at the swimming pool, stops at the post office and bank, explaining what the telephone repairman is doing up on the pole, reciting the days of the week, and reading books. To a child, the *quantity* of time is important."

Did you know that women who were classified as "satisfied homemakers" in one survey also scored highest on the adequacy of their mothering? [14]

On the other hand, "dissatisfied homemakers" made the worst mothers, according to the same survey. After studying six hundred women, three different researchers concluded that the most depressed group of women were mothers who wanted to work outside the home but did not.[15] For these women, it's easy to wonder if working outside the home might not have made them happier people, and thus, better parents.

Being a full-time stay-at-home mom is not everyone's choice, but it's clear that, for many women, it's the path of greatest fulfillment and least remorse. More often than we admit, it's a path that—with a little creativity—is financially possible.

Deborah Fallows concludes, at the end of her interview in *People:* "The 'need' to work varies enormously from person to person and often depends less on straightforward economic pressure than on material desires and individual definitions of success. Significantly, 47 percent of single mothers with children under the age of six are not in the work force, as opposed to only 23 percent of single mothers with older kids. That suggests that *even under the strongest economic pressure,* many women with very young children are deciding not to work."

There's no way around it. Dollars really *are* an issue for my family. I just wish there was some way I could work at home.

Even before Jenny got pregnant, both she and Jeff knew she would quit her full-time job as an accountant at the very first mention of Pampers on the grocery list.

She did, and those first months at home full-time with Mathew were priceless.

That is, before the financial squeeze began.

It was June, and Jeff—who teaches music classes at several local colleges—was home on summer vacation. Unfortunately, his paychecks from the various schools were also on vacation. To add to the financial bind, two of his private students had taken a leave of absence during the summer months, and his royalties from songwriting weren't making up the difference. The couple had just invested their nest egg in a Certificate of Deposit, and wouldn't have access to the money for a good six months.

The realization sank in: Summer was going to be a financial challenge.

Knowing that Jenny's time with Mathew was worth nearly any cost, the family tried to figure ways to boost their budget without sending her back to the office.

- They couldn't sell the second car because they didn't have one.

- They had already nixed high mortgage payments by choosing to live in an apartment.
- They weren't paying big bucks on any major loans or credit charges.
- They weren't extravagant with meals or entertainment.

One afternoon, as Jenny sat scratching her head over ways to bring in some extra dollars, Kaitlyn and I dropped in to visit. I was frustrated over the recent loss of the high-school girl I'd been paying to baby-sit Kaitlyn during my writing hours. Jenny was frustrated about, well, we already know what was ruining *her* day.

It was a match made in heaven. Jenny agreed to watch Kaitlyn in her home at the same rate I'd been paying the other baby sitter.

Before long, other working moms in the neighborhood began approaching Jenny with similar requests for child care. Her day-care center grew. Money problems shrank. By the time Jeff started teaching again in the fall, Jenny had a little business in full swing. And she'd done it all out of her own home.

Jenny's situation isn't unique. The U.S. Bureau of Labor Statistics estimates that eighteen million people are currently performing some income-producing work from their home. Some of these are among the growing number of moms launching their own businesses in search of flexible hours and/or opportunities to work at home. According to the Small Business Administration, right now women are going into business for themselves at *twice* the rate of men.

Other people are finding ways to keep their old jobs and still work at home. An article in *Family Policy,* a newsletter of the Family Research Council of America, reports that in November 1988, the Labor Department lifted a forty-five-year ban on home-based employment in five clothing industries. The move is expected to open up seventy-five thousand job opportunities for home-based workers.[16]

The article goes on to mention that the IBM Corporation recently announced a new program that will give employees with young children the chance to work from home. Computer modems, fax machines, and other communications technology are allowing employees from a growing number of industries to balance home life and office life from their very own living rooms.

If you're still not convinced that you can do it, consider these examples:

- When her three children were small, Linda ran a typing service out of an office in her garage. It brought in enough money for her single-income family and gave her the flexibility she needed to raise her kids.

- In order to spend my days with Kaitlyn and still bring in needed dollars, I've taken free-lance writing projects that have kept me writing through the night. There was also a period of time when I spent Saturdays canvassing my neighborhood, getting construction jobs for a contractor friend of ours. Until she started kindergarten this year, Kaitlyn spent several hours each week with a sitter so I could write during the day. Now that she's in school, I try to limit my work hours to the period of time she's gone. Oh, occasionally I call a friend and arrange an afternoon play-date for Kaitlyn so I can finish a project. But for the most part, my "home work" has allowed us to spend quality and quantity time together.

- Brenda Dalton—my cousin, friend, and a brand-new mother to boot—recently launched a home business designing maternity clothes for working women. Before that? Brenda worked at home—on commission—lining up paid speaking engagements for her dad and concert engagements for her husband, a talented musician.

- Dawn, a friend and associate who lives in California, used her home computer to launch a typesetting and desktop publishing business. She charges twenty dollars an hour and never leaves her kitchen table.

- Diane Watson turned a secondhand upright piano into extra cash for her family, teaching piano lessons to children from her neighborhood and church.

Finding just the right job may take all the creative problem-solving skills you can muster, but it's a livable alternative, especially when it's combined with careful budgeting and some material sacrifices. A growing number of working moms—particularly moms of young children—are discovering that, for their families, it's the only way to go.

I'd quit my job and take the plunge if I knew who I'd be once I hit the water. It's the dilemma of the missing identity.

I stood at the checkout stand at K-Mart. My shopping cart contained a baby thermometer, infant nose drops, a four-pack of pre-moistened Wipe'ems—and my six-week-old daughter asleep in her portable carrier. The cashier rang up my purchases, joked about which department carried the adorable sleeping babies, and then asked for my ID.

I whipped out my driver's license, check guarantee, Visa card, MasterCard, AAA card, Biola Alumni Association membership card, and the Red Cross card that states my blood type. (It was your typical afternoon in the express lane.)

And then it happened.

She asked for my work number.

I felt dizzy. My knees went weak. A slow burn started at my cheeks and worked its way into my scalp. My hands shook as I fumbled with my purse, trying to think of something to say. The truth was too awful—too awful even to speak. What if she could read it in my eyes? I squeezed my eyelids closed. I couldn't face it. I couldn't let her know—*I had no work number!*

I'd been on maternity leave for six weeks, and had used my old office number all that time, figuring I was "technically" still an employee even though I knew I wasn't going back to the office.

But all that had ended two days ago, on my last official day on the payroll. Maternity leave was over. So were my last ties to my identity as an employed, contributing member of society.

I had no work number. *I had no work number!*

The cashier was still staring. Waiting. Judging. I could practically hear the thoughts behind her beady little eyes: *She's probably one of those . . . those . . . whatever they're called. Those women who don't have a career. Those nonhumans who don't have a real title. What does she do all day, I wonder? Look at her. Her brain's already Cream of Wheat. She can't even answer a little question. Maybe if I asked it more simply. Maybe I could just get her to nod yes or no. . . .*

The cashier leaned toward me. "Do you have a work number?" she repeated slowly.

Suddenly something clicked in my mind and I chortled triumphantly. The cashier, still eyeing me, reached for the phone.

"Yes! Yes!" I blurted. "I'm a free-lance writer! I quit my job, but I'm still going to free-lance! Of course! That's a job. I'm working. I *have* a work number!"

The woman stared. "Good."

There was a long pause, like she was waiting for something. Then she said, "Can I have it, please?"

"Oh, yeah! Sure. It's . . . it's the same as my home number."

"Fine." The cashier scribbled something on the back of the check (a message for help, maybe?). Then she picked up the microphone to page someone for a check approval. Suddenly she changed her mind, hung up the mike, and handed me my receipt in a hurry.

I rushed to my car, a little embarrassed—but a whole lot relieved. I wasn't a nonhuman. I still had a job. Not just a "mom" job, but a professional job—one that paid real money.

To me, that meant I still had an identity.

Leaving full-time work means a drastic change in identity, and that's not an easy switch to make. But it can be an important step in developing our identity based on who we *are*, not just on what we *do*.

Here are a few suggestions for women who are leaving the rat race for a handful of precious little rug rats—and who are floundering over their change in identity. It's not such a scary switch if you do it in stages:

- ■ **Stay involved—on a paid or volunteer basis—with something that expresses your interests or values.** During my first year home with Kaitlyn, I was active in a local pro-life group. This gave me an avenue to express my values and concerns and kept me in touch with an issue I had pursued professionally when I helped write a book on abortion.

■ **Keep informed on the issues of the day.** Part of my identity had been the interesting projects I'd been involved with and could therefore discuss. I was terrified of becoming someone who couldn't discuss anything beyond diaper rash and teething remedies.

■ **Don't be afraid to expand your identity with new friendships and activities.** Part of my fear of losing my "work self" was simply a fear of the unknown. I was plunging into an unknown body of water, and I wasn't sure I'd find any other fish like myself. I soon discovered other women with whom I could identify, full-time mothers as well as women like myself who were managing the home front while keeping a foot in the career door by dabbling in their profession.

Self-identity is a complex issue affected by, among other things, how we spend our time, our values and how we live them out, positive feedback from peers and authority figures, events from our pasts. I can't tell you there isn't an adjustment period for women who drastically restructure their lives, but like all adjustment periods, it's temporary. Just knowing it's going to be there—and that you're not the only person getting the shakes in the checkout line—can help ease the trauma.

And if that advice doesn't help, rent a P.O. box. It's almost as good as having a work number.

Dealing with feelings
of getting left behind.

I interviewed Drs. Pamela Addison and Leslie Brown at Leslie's home in Pasadena. Both psychologists recently took their practices to quarter-time to accommodate motherhood. During the interview, Pamela's daughter, Melissa, eighteen months, and Leslie's six-month-old daughter, Ashley, shared responsibilities for cooing into the recorder microphone, threatening to grind lipstick into Leslie's oriental rug, and chewing on blank cassette tapes. As the doting mother of a precious little girl who used to excel at very similar activities, I admit I was delighted by the whole process.

Yet the interview took a serious turn when I asked the women if they ever felt left behind professionally since going part-time to care for their infants.

Pamela, an energetic brunette with a boyish face and a California tan, answered frankly. "I do," she admitted. "All the time. Partly because, in the last year, three out of ten members of my close peer group have all gone on to post-graduate training—which is something I desperately want to do—and my husband is going next year. I'm not the leader of the pack anymore. Everyone is beginning to pass me by. I have no doubt that I'm going to attain these professional goals, but I have to wait, and that's what I'm struggling with. I'm trying to learn how to wait in a way that is not begrudging."

Leslie, on the other hand, admitted that she felt guilty over the fact that she *didn't* feel left behind. While post-graduate work and similar professional milestones were her goals as well, she said it wouldn't matter all that much if she *never* got around to them. She and her husband had waited ten years for Ashley, and, at this point, she was content to see clients quarter-time and spend the rest of her time enjoying her daughter.

The transition had been relatively easy for her, but not so easy for her friend.

Pamela added, "When I start to feel left behind, I remind myself that I made a choice based on what I believe about Melissa's development and her needs. I have two callings: One is to be a good wife and parent; the other is to do my job. It's not as if one calling matters and the other doesn't, but one calling *is* more important. My job is secondary, and I could give it up tomorrow for reasons related to my health, Melissa's health, her needs, or my husband's needs.

"Yet I work because I *love* what I do. And there *are* times it would be nice to be married yet single, with my life and my time my own to invest in my career like I did before Randy and I became a family. And *that's* when I envy what other people have. *That's* when I feel left behind. Those carefree days are gone, and I have to keep readjusting to that."

At that moment, blonde-haired Melissa toddled toward Pamela, who was sitting cross-legged on the floor. Melissa turned and backed into her mother, dropping her diapered bottom onto Pamela's lap and snuggling into ready arms. Pamela smiled. "When push comes to shove, I'd much rather be with Melissa. I'm glad I made the choice I did. But it doesn't mean the feelings go away. Every time I get the desire to do some of the things I've postponed for Melissa, I have to work it through again and again. The feelings don't get settled once and for all. It's a constant process of counting the costs of the decision I made and weighing them against the alternative."

If I take the plunge,
can I ever *"un*plunge"?

Ann was in her office, drinking decaf and scanning the morning paper, when something caught her attention. A local women's association was sponsoring a seminar for working women. The title of the seminar, printed in bold, black letters across the face of a tiny boxed ad, struck at Ann's heart like a dagger: "How to Break Back into the Career Market: It Doesn't Necessarily Take a Miracle."

Ann winced. *Is that where I'm headed? If I quit my job, if I drop out of the fast lane, can I ever get back in? Or will I end up parked on the soft shoulder forever?*

Ann jumped as the door to her office flew open. Mitch, leaning on the doorknob, hung in the entry. "Come on! Come on! He's on his way up the stairs right now!"

Ann gasped. "Mitch! You scared the tar out of me. Why are you always so hyper? Even hot coffee doesn't do that to a person—unless someone dumps it in your lap. Just calm down."

"Hurry out here and play politics or I'll carry you out," Mitch warned.

Ann looked down at her body, eight months pregnant, and smiled. "You and who else?"

Just then Ann's intercom buzzed and the voice of the agency receptionist filled the little office.

"Ann, Mr. Denning just arrived with several other members of the board. They're ready to present the commendation. Everyone's meeting in the conference room."

Mitch beamed. "See? See? And it was all your work. Your stuff on the Paradise Burger account was great. Just great.

You're unstoppable. A sheer dynamo in the office. You're going straight to the top, Ann. Straight to the top."

Ann crumpled the newspaper and held it at arm's length over the trash basket. She had almost made the decision to let it drop when Mitch interrupted the process.

"Stop stalling! Hurry! Let's go!" he urged.

"Hold your horses! They're not little gods in there."

"No, but they're the board. And some of 'em *think* they're next to deity."

Ann stared at the crumpled ball in her hand. Suddenly she drew the paper back to her desk. Maybe she hadn't made a decision yet, after all. She smoothed the wrinkled pages, taking a last glance at the little boxed ad with the bold, black headlines. Then she heaved herself up out of her chair.

"Okay, Mr. Patience. Let's go meet the board."

Can women drop out of the career race, take a five- to twenty-year maternity sabbatical, then jump back in before the race ends and the janitor shows up to collect the litter? The views are mixed.

"We can't all be Geraldine Ferraro and take thirteen years out, become a full-time mother, then jump in and be a lawyer and politician. Taking time out can cause permanent damage. You never resurrect your career or your earning power," claims Sylvia Ann Hewlett, author of *A Lesser Life: The Myth of Women's Liberation in America.*

According to an article in *Business Weekly*: "Only about 2 percent of corporate officers at major public companies are women. About 60 percent of top female executives do not have children, while 95 percent of the men do. The message seems clear: If you're a mother, don't bother."[17]

On the other hand, retired executive Phyllis Sewell writes: "Fortunately, 26 years ago my employer, Federated Department Stores, Inc., was far-sighted enough to realize the advantages of a part-time executive and let me work three days a week while our son was young. My career was on a plateau for a few years, but in the decade following my return to full-time employment, I received three significant promotions."[18]

According to Sylvia Nash, director of the national Christian Management Association (CMA): "The world is open these days to providing more for the mother at home as well as for the woman who needs to function at home and at the office. Because, after all, there's going to come a period of time when a child no longer requires full-time attention, and Mom returns to the work force a hundred percent. She hasn't lost any of her skills. And if she continued to keep updated regarding the organization, she's right back in full speed."[19]

Arlene Rossen Cardozo, mother of three, calls it "sequencing" (she is the author of a book by the same name). "Sequencing," she argues, "combines the best of modern feminism with the best of traditional mothering."

According to the experts, sequencing simply means accepting life in stages and knowing when to place a career on hold for the benefits of home life. And, according to some of the moms who have tried it, sequencing is the ultimate in creative problem solving. It also means—finally, truly, and sanely—being able to "have it all."

Ann let herself in the front door around nine-thirty in the evening. She had called ahead, so Rick knew to come straight home from work, relieve the baby sitter, and go ahead with dinner.

She hollered out a greeting as she peeled off her jacket and hung it in the hall closet. Only the TV answered her, although the smell of hot dogs and macaroni lingered in the air.

"Rick? Brittney?"

Still carrying her briefcase, Ann walked through the kitchen, past a pile of unwashed pots and dishes, and on into the den. Rick and Brittney lay sleeping in front of the TV, propped up together in the tattered bean bag from Rick's college days.

A cable rerun of "The Waltons" was just ending. Ann flipped off the tube, nestled into an easy chair, and sat watching her little family. It was time for some thinking—and for some prayer.

The house was silent now, except for Rick's heavy breathing and for one moment when Brittney stirred. The only other sound came from the rhythm of the pendulum clock on the mantel: *tick tock tick tock. . . .*

Slow. Measured. Paced. There was a balance in the pace, and each beat held the promise of the next. The old clock kept the beat of time. It kept the heartbeat of the house.

Maybe life had a rhythm, too. A pace. A balance. A cadence of birth and death, grief and joy, struggle and triumph, waiting and having, doing and being.

There was time for it all. Sooner or later—some now and some then.

As soon as Rick woke up, she would tell him her decision.

Ann had career success; today's recognition said it all. She'd proven herself to the world, to her family, to the board, and even to herself. But lately she'd been struggling and striving and clutching and grabbing, against the rhythm, out of sync. The pendulum would swing again. There would be time again for the world she'd be leaving. Time to stage a comeback. Time to dust off her briefcase and her Day Timer. She didn't know when, but she knew she would know at the time. And it would be the right time.

It was after ten. Rick and Brittney still slept on the floor. Ann pursed her lips. Should she wake them, or let them sleep where they lay? Ann spotted the afghan on the couch. One hand on her taut stomach, she struggled to her feet and reached for the blanket.

She heard a soft *thud.*

She'd knocked over her briefcase with her foot.

A moment later Rick and Brittney were warmly covered. Ann picked up her briefcase and headed toward the spare room she'd turned into an office. There were a couple of files she needed to review.

Five minutes passed.

Ten.

Fifteen minutes later the briefcase had yet to be opened. Instead, Ann—dressed in maternity sweats and hugging a couple of pillows and a faded quilt—padded down the hall toward the den where Rick and Brittney slept.

It was time to join the family.

Notes

1. Margaret Jaworski and Robin Sanders, "Going Home," *Ladies' Home Journal* (October 1988).

2. Lesley Jane Nonkin, "Catch-28," *Working Woman* (May 1987).

3. "Do Kids Need a Stay-at-Home Mom?" *Redbook* magazine survey results (August 1986).

4. Bee-Lan C. Wang and Richard J. Stellway, *Should You Be the Working Mom?* (Elgin, Ill.: David C. Cook Publishing Co., 1987), p. 29.

5. Jaworski and Sanders, "Going Home."

6. Author's interview with Debbie Shakarian.

7. Jaworski and Sanders, "Going Home."

8. Survey Results—Mark Clements Research, Inc.

9. "Do Kids Need a Stay-at-Home Mom?"

10. "The Family in America," The Rockford Institute, Rockford, Ill. (September 1988).

11. Labor Letter, *Wall Street Journal* (May 23, 1989).

12. "Do Kids Need a Stay-at-Home Mom?"

13. Deborah Fallows, "When Both Parents Work," *People* (July 1987), p. 42.

14. Wang and Stellway, *Should You Be the Working Mom?*, p. 73.

15. Ibid., p. 94.

16. William R. Mattox, Jr., "Giving Parents More Homework," *Family Policy*, a publication of the Family Research Council of America (November/December 1988).

17. Elizabeth Ehrlich, "Is the Mommy Track a Blessing—or a Betrayal?" *Business Weekly* (May 15, 1989).

18. Ibid.

19. Author's interview with Sylvia Nash.

13

Affair Prevention and Recovery

Falling Out of Love with the Other Man:
When Work Relationships
Get Too Close

Forty-two percent of working women surveyed
admitted to having had an affair.
Only 27 percent of nonworking women
admitted making the same mistake.[1]

Mrs. Feinberg died two days before Thanksgiving. Christine took it hard.

"It's not just the death," said Christine. While covering the phones at the nurses' station, she shared her grief with a male intern. "God knows death is old news around here. Maybe it was the suddenness. An hour ago she was showing me pictures of her grandkids."

The intern nodded. "Strokes don't give much warning."

Christine sighed. "We were becoming friends."

Later that morning Christine was on her way to the cafeteria when she passed Nick Nicholson near the lab. The doctor fell into step beside her.

"You okay?" he asked.

"Me? Sure. Why?"

"I mean, about Mrs. Feinberg. I know you really liked her."

"Yes. And she really liked you."

The young doctor looked surprised. "Oh? She always seemed 'put off' when I saw her."

Christine smiled. "Okay, so she didn't *like* you. But she thought you were good-looking. She told me so."

"Incredible." Nick chuckled, shaking his head.

Christine turned and stared. "Why's that so incredible? She was old, but she still had eyes. You *are* good-looking." A moment later she retraced her words. "Oh! Oh, I'm sorry. I shouldn't have said . . . " She paused, then grinned.

"What's so funny?"

"You're red. You're blushing."

"And that's funny?"

"No, it isn't funny." Christine hid a smile. "It's interesting, but it's not funny. I'm sorry. I'm not paying attention to what I'm saying. I'm still—I don't know—I'm still *weird* over what happened this morning. I really liked the old woman. She was like a . . . like a mom. A little like my mom, in fact."

"Is your mom still living?"

"No. She died four years ago, right around Valentine's Day, in a hospital, not a whole lot different from this one. Heart failure. And I wasn't there. I was . . . Where *was* I? Somewhere pointless, I'm sure. I arrived an hour too late. I've never forgiven myself for that."

"Christine—"

Christine smacked her palm into her forehead. "I'm rambling. Enough said. I'm sorry."

Nick watched Christine with eyes that smiled. "You say you're sorry a lot, you know that?"

"I know. The nurturer side of me. I have to make everything okay for everyone else. I read about it in a book once."

"Look. Were you on your way to lunch?" Nick asked.

Christine nodded.

"So am I. You've still got forty-five minutes. Let's hit some-place on the outside, take a *real* break from this place."

That evening when Dan came home from his job at the accounting firm, Christine greeted him at the door. She told him about Mrs. Feinberg, about the photos of the grandkids, and even how the death evoked memories of her mother.

The one thing she didn't mention—and she wasn't quite sure why—was Nick.

Why women in the workplace are vulnerable to affairs.

Over half the married people in this country admit to having had at least one extramarital affair.

That fact is startling enough.

Now add all the men and women, married or single, who have nurtured illicit relationships in their hearts, minds, or words, regardless of whether or not those relationships were ever consummated between the sheets. The exact number, if we knew it, would be mind-boggling.

The fact is, no man or woman is immune to the ecstasies and agonies of dangerous liaisons. Today's working woman may be particularly vulnerable. It's a fact that significantly more working women than stay-at-home moms become involved in extramarital relationships or entertain the possibility of doing so.

Why? Why are we so vulnerable to affairs?

Exposure is one reason. For eight hours each day, five days a week, we're exposed to countless numbers of relationships with male coworkers, bosses, clients, vendors, patients, subordinates, laborers, consultants, etc. Couple this kind of exposure with the next factor, *transition in the workplace*, and you've got an explosive combination.

Transition in the workplace is a factor because one generation ago women weren't a major influence in the office. It's only been in the past twenty years that women have begun carving a place for themselves in the hallowed halls of a realm previously reserved for men. This means, at many corporate levels, women and men are still adjusting to each other in a lot of areas, including gender roles, stereotypes, gender-related skills and strengths, and sexuality. When women introduced themselves in great numbers to the work force, the opportunities for sexual chemistry between coworkers shot sky-high as well.

Linda and I believe our society is still figuring out how to respond to increased sexuality in the workplace. The battle to recognize, define, and discourage sexual harassment is one indication that the transition is still under way. Affairs are yet another sign.

Exposure. Transition. Now consider a third factor: *professional intimacy.*

The workplace often throws people together in professionally intense or creative settings. We're asked to solve problems, meet organizational goals . . . face challenges, create proposals, meet deadlines. Adrenaline flows, the clock ticks, brains storm. More adrenaline flows. Sweat pours. Anxiety gnaws. There might be shared lunches or late nights at the office. A bond is forged between colleagues who share a challenge, share the sweat, and share the triumph.

When a man and a woman find themselves in this kind of situation, the intensity of emotions created by the project can become transferred onto the working partner. Professional chemistry can give way to sexual chemistry, and men and women struggling to put a problem to bed can find their bodies quickly following suit.

Exposure. Transition. Professional intimacy.

And then there's a fourth dynamic. It's this little thing called *emotional need*. The stress and pressures of holding down two full-time jobs (one that pays and one that doesn't) can create areas of need that leave women vulnerable to the lure of romantic entanglements.

- ■ If we feel overworked, we may be tempted to consider the escape promised by a heady fling.

- ■ If we feel unappreciated at home or at the office, we may be vulnerable to the compliments of a handsome coworker.

- ■ If we feel as though we're always running ten steps behind, failing miserably at the task of being Superwoman, then it might seem like a welcome change to venture into an illicit arena where our efforts meet with "success."

- ■ If we are married to men who don't appreciate our professional interests or contributions, we may find ourselves attracted to men at work who do.

- ■ If we feel overwhelmed by the incredible responsibilities at home and at work, we may be all the more ready to exchange our grown-up burdens for the kind of romantic rush and blush we felt when we were sixteen, and the world lay at our doorstep.

Exposure. Transition. Professional intimacy. Emotional needs. And, finally, *setting*.

Men and women in the workplace invest the best hours of their day on the job. We're at our wittiest and our prettiest.

We're on our best behavior. We look our best. We feel our best. We do our best. For eight hours every day, we present an image, an image we don't have to keep up (nor would we have the energy to do so) when we go home at night. The workplace is a slice of our day and of ourselves—and it's usually the best piece of the pie.

Is it any wonder, then, that we might attract—and become attracted to—someone under these kinds of circumstances?

Is *your* heart in danger?
Know the signs.

Two months after her lunch with Nick, Christine knew she had a crush on the handsome blond doctor.

She hadn't had an inkling at first.

During the weeks immediately following their impromptu lunch, she had actually believed she was walking past his office at lunchtime just because it broke the routine path she usually took to the cafeteria.

She had almost managed to deny the fact that she was lingering in the daily care of Nick's patients, with the subtle hope that he might make his rounds while she was there.

And she had nearly convinced herself that the new makeup she'd purchased on a whim was nothing more than that—a whim.

But two months after sharing burgers with Nick, Christine couldn't deny the signs any longer. She was infatuated with the man.

Is *your* heart in danger?

For just a moment, don't be put off by the word *affair*. And don't look for the obvious signs of an affair (such as motel receipts or your lipstick on his collar). After all, an affair doesn't happen overnight. It's a process beginning in the secret places of the heart and mind. If you shrug off a warning sign just because it doesn't include a word or a touch, you're begging for trouble.

According to Peter Kreitler:

> Extramarital relationships—both adulterous and non-sexual—can destroy the best of marriages. It might be a one-night stand at a Chicago convention between two people who meet, share drinks and dinner conversation, make love, and part company forever. Or it could be an emotional or intellectual friendship that lasts for months or even years without sex ever occurring.[2]

Consider the red flags:

- Do you find yourself making special trips past the desk of a male coworker, or going out of your way to put yourself in the path of someone interesting at work? It may even be a boss or someone else with whom you're legitimately pursuing a project. Do you find yourself relishing reasons to make contact?
- Have you taken new interest in what you wear and how you look?
- Is there a friend or coworker who makes you feel like you're sixteen again?
- We all struggle with the temptation of immoral thoughts, most of them fleeting. But are your thoughts drawn *repeatedly* to anyone special, other than your spouse? Or, if you're single, to someone you can't date—like someone married?
- Do you find yourself looking forward to the meetings or events where a certain person will be in attendance? Long before you mentally admit having

an attraction to someone, you may find yourself attracted to the places you'll be likely to see him.

- When you talk about your work with family, friends, or husband, how do you talk about the person to whom you're attracted? Like Christine, do you find yourself "forgetting" to mention seemingly innocent interactions with the other man? Or do you find yourself drawn by opportunities to talk about him, or about meetings or projects in which he's involved? Either approach is a bright red flag.

- When you think about that person, do you find yourself justifying the relationship to yourself with thoughts like, *We're just friends* ...

- Do you justify the relationship to yourself—and to others—with facts that are unrelated to the real issue?

  We interviewed a woman whose sister was the first to suspect that the woman was considering an affair with her boss. The sister asked pointblank, "Is there something going on between you two?" The woman protested, "Are you serious? He's married with four kids." The sister was wise enough to respond, "That's not the question I asked." The fact that someone's married and/or has kids has *no* bearing on how he may impact your heart.

- Has your prayer life gone cold? Are you as eager to read the Word and go to church, or do these things feel like they've lost their relevance?

- What about your music? Do sexy lyrics or melancholy love songs hold a new fascination? Do they pose a backdrop for new feelings of sensuality or thoughts of another man?

- Do you welcome opportunities to share a touch—no matter how innocent? A friend of mine, who was working for a Christian firm, attended an office chapel with a coworker to whom she was attracted. The highlight of the morning came when the speaker asked the employees to join hands and pray. You can bet that dialogue with God was the last thing on my friend's mind when the man next to her entwined his hand in hers.

The $64,000 question is not, "*Will* I ever be attracted to someone I can't have?" The real question is, "*When* it happens, what am I going to do about it?"

Outside the hospital, the snow fell thickly. Inside, Christine sat in the nurses' lounge, sipping a diet Coke and pondering her crush on Nick. She thought about telling a friend from church, just to hear some sound biblical advice. She considered telling her husband, to take the "secretive edge" off her feelings. She thought about bringing Dan's picture to work and setting it at the nurses' station where she'd see it often and be reminded of the man she loved. She wondered if she should reroute her path to lunch to purposely avoid running into Nick. She played with the idea of making her "schoolgirl" crush a matter of prayer.

But in the end, she simply shrugged away her concerns. After all, it wasn't like she was having an affair, or even thinking about it. The couple of times each day when Christine ran into Nick, the encounters were warm but professional. No onlooker would ever guess what she was feeling. Her actions—and her words—had been irreproachable. Besides, they were just friends. She hadn't done anything wrong.

Three weeks later, in February, Christine took the boys to the shopping mall. The two older ones disappeared into the arcade gallery. Pushing Paulie in the stroller, Christine headed into a bookstore to find something for Dan for Valentine's Day.

Nothing seemed particularly interesting in the bookstore. She strolled Paulie past a candy shop (Dan was trying to lose five pounds, so she couldn't stop there), and past an automotive parts outlet (Dan would be pleased, but Christine couldn't think of anything less romantic). She paused at a lingerie boutique and peered through the window at lacy nightwear in shades of fire-engine red, passion pink, and midnight black. That might be fun . . .

Then she wheeled the stroller around and headed back for the unromantic auto shop. She wasn't sure why, but in the depths of her heart, she suspected it had something to do with her growing feelings for Nick.

On Valentine's Day, Christine returned from lunch and found a card and a single rosebud waiting for her at the nurses' station. She opened the card gingerly, her heart pounding inside her chest. The message was scrawled in an unfamiliar hand:

> *You told me your mother died around Valentine's Day. You didn't mention the exact day, but I figured this time of year might hold some sad memories for you. I hope this rose is a bright spot in your day.*
>
> Nick

Throughout her afternoon rounds, Christine kept an eye open for Nick, to thank him for the rose. The two finally spotted each other in the hallway around three in the afternoon, just before Christine went home for the day. They stood off to one side, talking in low voices. Christine was smiling and looking up at the doctor. At one point Nick touched her shoulder lightly as he spoke. After fifteen minutes, Christine glanced at her watch and squealed. She backed away from Nick, explaining something briefly. He nodded. Then she tore down the hall, toward the parking lot, and home to the family that had somehow slipped her mind.

Near the end of February, Nick invited Christine to lunch. She hesitated briefly before nodding her assent. On the way back from the coffee shop, Nick fell silent in the car.

"Is something wrong?" Christine probed.

"No. Well, actually, yes."

"Can you tell me about it?" Christine's palms were sweaty.

"I wish I could, Christine," Nick said. "But maybe we shouldn't talk about it."

"Maybe we should," Christine answered, staring out the passenger window. Her heart was pounding triple-time in her chest.

"Nothing can happen, Christine," Nick blurted. "We've got to promise each other. Nothing can happen."

Christine nodded. She didn't pretend she didn't know what Nick was referring to. "I promise," she said weakly.

Christine hoped the brief conversation might strengthen her resolve. But the only thing the secret promise managed to do was strengthen the bond between them.

How can something that feels so good be so destructive?

In preparing this chapter, Linda and I interviewed four women who know firsthand the ecstasy and agony of losing their hearts to the wrong men—and the struggle of reclaiming what was lost.

When remembering their illicit relationships, all four women spoke of feelings that were too good to ignore: excitement, romance, appreciation, chemistry, companionship, intellectual and emotional compatibility, even spiritual closeness. And all four spoke of incredible personal torment.

Joanne, a single working mother who fell in love with a married colleague, said, "For single parents, there's often a total void of romance or sexuality. So for me, it felt *good* to spend time with a man. But it was this Jekyll-and-Hyde kind of thing. The torment came with trying to reconcile my values with feelings that were out of control."

She added: "Sometimes the torment came when we were together, like when he invited me and my kids to spend Christmas Day with his family. His kids treated me like an aunt, and his wife treated me like a friend. And he seemed very caring and attentive to his family. Yet all the while my emotions contrasted drastically with the family scene being played out before me. It was very painful, and very difficult to accept that they had something I didn't have in my single-parent family. The emotional pain was almost tangible."

Beth Ann is the mother of two high-school boys. When she went to work part-time in her church office, she soon found herself drawn to Tony, an assistant pastor who shared her passion for Christian education.

"He was very attractive, with a buoyant personality," she remembers. "And he had a quick wit and tremendous sense of humor. It began pretty innocently when I was at church working and we were discussing some curriculum. It was getting close to lunch and we weren't done. He suggested we finish talking over lunch. I then suggested we call my husband,

Steve, who taught one of the Sunday school classes we were discussing, and have him join us.

"But Steve was having a business lunch and couldn't come. During lunch Tony asked if Steve and I could help drive the youth group to a film on Sunday night. I said sure. But on Sunday night, Steve couldn't go, so I went alone. When Tony and I dropped the kids off at church, he asked me to wait a minute. I remember sitting on the hood of my car, waiting for the kids to leave, and waiting for Tony. I felt like a high-schooler again. We stood in the parking lot and talked and talked, long after the kids were gone and the church lights were dimmed. I remember thinking, *I'm really enjoying this person. I can't wait to see him again.* A red flag went up. These were new feelings. The next day he called me at home with a question about work. Before long, we were talking every day, either at the office or by phone on the days I didn't go to work.

"I became very frightened. I thought, *This person means an awful lot to me.* I enjoyed talking to him more than my other friends. Tony began saying things with a double meaning, things like, 'You really light up my day.' I wasn't used to hearing those kinds of compliments. Something was beginning to feel not as neutral as it was before. I remember the first time he said, 'I really love you.' We were in a restaurant, and I almost choked on my sandwich. You know, Christians say that all the time. But I picked up a double meaning. I was scared, but really excited. And I couldn't back out of it. It felt too good to have this person in my life.

"My husband, Steve, now was beginning to question, 'Why are you spending so much time with this person?' I kept telling him Tony was important in my life and that we were just friends. And all the while I was thinking, *I'm a Christian. I'm on top of things. I'm not sure I know what's going on, but whatever it is, I can handle it.*

"Tony and I talked about spiritual things, so I figured the relationship had to be okay. I even praised God for sending me such a wonderful Christian friend. But deep down I knew things weren't okay. And Tony *wasn't* a gift from God.

"After a couple of months, Tony and I were both admitting the fact that we had a very involved relationship with one another. We loved each other but talked about loving our spouses, too. At no time did we ever refer to our relationship as an affair. We told ourselves this was a deep, spiritual relationship. We couldn't face the reality; therefore, we tried to dress it up as something acceptable.

"By now he was calling me at home twice a day, even on the half-days I saw him at the office. We looked for ways to get away from everyone, just to kiss and hold each other. Yet we still denied it was an affair.

"Steve was getting more concerned about it. One night he told me, 'I don't want you to see Tony anymore.' I managed to weasel out of the argument without any promises. But inside, I was furious at the thought. I thought to myself, *You've got to be kidding. This is the most important person in my life.* At times, when I would get a glimpse of where this could end, it was really scary.

"It was no small miracle when Steve came home and told me he'd requested a job transfer and we were moving to Ohio. Part of me was frantic at the news. But deep down part of me was relieved, because I knew I was out of control. I was too weak to recognize the situation for what it was, take control, and get out. I needed someone to do that for me.

"Eight weeks later we moved. Tony and I wrote letters back and forth. I thought that was safe. Yet Steve and I still argued about it. Steve would yell, 'It doesn't make sense that a *friend* would write several times a week. Wake up, Beth Ann! This is more like a college romance than a friendship!' Twice I tried to sneak Tony's letters into the trash can before

Steve could find them. But both times, when the trash man emptied the can, Tony's letters somehow remained stuck to the side or bottom of the can. Steve found them both times. He was furious. Did I feel guilty? Actually, no. I was still in too much denial.

"After six months, Steve came home and announced, 'I went to the doctor.' I asked if he was sick. He said. 'No. I've been to a counselor. He wants you to come, too.'"

Beth Ann remembers that, in counseling, she finally faced the fact that she and Tony were involved in an affair. That's when the torment began.

"I thought I would fall apart," she says. "I remember being in the shower and suddenly feeling so panicky I had to get out of the shower, get dressed, and take a drive. I was panicked at seeing my dark side. It was overwhelming. Very frightening.

"I remember another time being afraid to go to the gynecologist for my annual checkup. I figured he was going to find a lump in my breast because somehow, in my twisted reasoning, I thought I deserved it. Time and time again, I had to deal with a lot of harsh reality.

"For a long time, I kept thinking that if only I'd had someone—even a book—say to me, 'These are things that can happen in a marriage, these are symptoms, these are signs, this is what it will feel like, but it's a lie. . . . ' If only I'd had a tool at the front end to say Christians aren't infallible; when you think you're strong, you aren't . . . Then maybe at the very beginning I could have said, 'I remember reading about this,' and Steve and I would have gone to counseling then, before all the damage was done."

Beth Ann says that, six years later, she and Steve still live with the scars. Steve's relationship with God is rocky; he's still angry that God allowed another man to threaten his marriage in such a manner.

They live with the pain, but Beth Ann has finally learned to move past the guilt. She remembers one evening, months into counseling and after repeated apologies to Steve and to God: "Steve was really upset. Really angry. Every night was a shouting match as he struggled to resolve what had happened in our marriage. And his accusations just fueled my own: How could I have been so blind? How could I have hurt Steve so much? How could I, as a Christian, have fallen so far?

"One night I just couldn't take it anymore. I yelled back at Steve, 'I am sick and tired of you being so angry. I've asked your forgiveness. I've asked God's forgiveness. What more do you want me to do?'

"Steve fumed. He said, 'There's got to be more. There's got to be punishment. Someone's got to pay for what you did.'

"Suddenly it hit me. I looked at my husband and said, 'Somebody did.'

"And that fact sank into my heart for the very first time, after months of torment and repentance. Christ had paid for this. I was forgiven. In forgiveness, there is no punishment, but there are consequences. Steve and I are still living with the consequences of my sin. But God's been with us through the consequences. We're finally rebuilding our lives."

Are we actually in love with another man . . . or in love with a missing piece in our lives?

During fourteen years of marriage, Christine had been the giver, the nurturer. She'd planned all the special family moments, organized the holidays, created the memories for the entire family.

She loved her husband. But she'd often felt a void left by one single missing piece in their relationship. She'd wished a zillion times that Dan would take more initiative in demonstrating his care for her.

These thoughts and others waged war within her soul as Christine paced the sidewalk fronting the city park just blocks from the hospital. She pulled her coat tighter around her body. Despite subtle signs of spring—snow thawing into muddy slush, longer days, scattered green buds appearing on stark and naked tree limbs—a chill edge remained in the air, and Christine was ice-cold. She hoped she didn't have to wait long.

Christine's internal battle clamored for her attention. She sighed. She felt incredibly guilty, but Nick gave her the very thing she lacked from Dan. He had been concerned about Christine's feelings when Mrs. Feinberg died. He remembered the anniversary of Christine's mother's death. He initiated lunches, dropped anonymous notes in Christine's locker, and looked for her in the halls as much as she looked for him. For the first time in a long time, Christine was receiving something back—and she didn't even have to arrange it for herself. It was spontaneous, a gift from another human being. It felt wonderful.

"Christine?"

She whirled toward the voice behind her. A man in a navy blue wool coat stood watching her. Nick smiled, and Christine's heart turned to water in her chest. She moved quickly into his arms and their mouths met in a kiss.

Joanne, the single working mother we mentioned a few pages back, remembered that her relationship with a married friend had filled a void existing in her fatherless home.

And, according to Beth Ann, her illicit relationship with Tony seemed to complement her relationship with her husband, Steve. "The gaps in our marriage were being filled by another person," she remembers. "Suddenly I had the total package. *All* my needs were being met. My relationship with

Steve seemed to improve because I wasn't frustrated, unhappy, hungry."

The simple fact is this:

Affairs are *not* relationships between whole persons. They are relationships between a need and a fantasy.

Illicit relationships are simply a way of coping with a "missing piece" in the puzzle of our lives or marriages. If we find that "missing piece" in another man, we may be tempted to build the image of a complete, whole, perfect lover from that one single piece. In reality, we aren't in love with a man; we're in love with a fantasy.

Norm Wright, in *Seasons of a Marriage*, writes:

> Many [people] actually marry their own physical and emotional need. They have a personal need to be cared for, to be happy, to have economic security, to become a parent, etc. They create an image of a person who they think will be able to meet these needs and then marry their invented image.[3]

If some marriages are relationships between images, affairs are even more so.

This book is dedicated to helping working women get past the "roles" and segmentation of their lives, and begin living and thinking as whole, integrated persons. Illicit relationships—including ones that exist only in the heart as well as full-blown affairs—force each partner to interact with only a small sliver of himself or herself. Affairs don't require interaction between two whole people; in fact, the whole person just gets in the way.

One woman we interviewed recalled a conversation she'd had with the coworker she was involved with. She asked him if he ever thought about her when he was home with his family. He told her he tried to segment his life into little boxes and attempted to keep his illicit romance from impacting the box he called "family life."

Another woman was shocked to learn that Gerald, the man she'd been involved with for two years, was, with his wife, expecting a baby. She felt betrayed that the tiny segment of Gerald she'd managed to fill out into a whole person was, in reality, still a small segment. She didn't possess the whole Gerald. For that matter, she didn't even *know* the whole Gerald.

The world recently observed the fiftieth anniversary of *Gone with the Wind*. I doubt there's a one of us unfamiliar with Ashley Wilkes and Scarlett O'Hara. Scarlett manages to build the image of a larger-than-life lover from a dreamer named Ashley Wilkes. The bulk of their relationship exists only in Scarlett's mind, yet her obsession colors her life for more than a decade. To spite Ashley, Scarlett marries a man she doesn't love. Later, her fantasies come between her and Ashley's wife, the only real friend Scarlett ever had. Eventually, her mental affair with Ashley threatens to destroy her marriage to Rhett Butler, the true man of her dreams.

In the last moments of the movie, Scarlett realizes that Ashley is little more than a shadow of the man she thought she knew and loved. She realizes she has been in love with an image, while Ashley has been merely infatuated with Scarlett's colorful zest for life. It's an awesome insight—too late to save Scarlett's marriage to Rhett—but nonetheless timed by moviemakers to deliver a dramatic punch and add clarity in hindsight to the epic tale.

Few can forget the image of Scarlett collapsed with grief on the sweeping staircase of her empty Atlanta mansion. Her devastation is complete as she realizes her affair with an image has cost her the love of a real man.

But that's nothing compared to what it feels like in real life.

The first step in getting out: Seeing the whole picture.

It's impossible to escape the steely grasp of an illicit relationship as long as we're caught up in the rosy image we've created. The first step in getting out is taking a long, cold look at reality.

- For Joanne, the whole picture emerged as she began to notice character flaws in the married man she adored. Where he had once been perfect, she began to see several cracks and faults. Eventually she saw enough reality to go to work reclaiming her heart.

- For another woman I'll call Shirley, constant fantasies about a male friend seemed harmless—until she took a good look at her marriage and discovered that, even without the physical presence of another man in her life, she'd been drifting from her husband. Shirley woke up to the fact that her lustful thoughts about an imaginary lover were robbing her of a *real* relationship with the *real* man in her life.

- Beth Ann couldn't see the whole picture until Steve dragged her to marriage counseling. Once there, the realization hit her like a summer thunderstorm: her fine, spiritual relationship was a deceptive affair. A year's worth of denial slipped away, like mud and sludge slipping down a storm drain. When she finally took a good hard look at herself, stripped of excuses and drenched in sin, she was grief-stricken at the sight.

But it was reality. And it was truth. And it was the first step back to wholeness.

Part of seeing the whole picture is recognizing the costs. Here are just a few of the costs of illicit relationships:[4]

- living with lying
- feelings of guilt
- avoidance of marriage problems
- looking for faults in your spouse as a way of justifying the affair
- manipulating close friends who are asked to help keep your secret
- the ripple effect of a broken marriage, which leaves a gaping void in the lives of children, relatives, and friends of the one-time couple
- lack of energy for anything other than the affair

If all else fails, consider these ramifications, which aren't at all unlikely:

- the possibility of contracting venereal disease, including AIDS
- the risk of losing your job if an intraoffice affair comes to light
- potential physical retaliation by an irate spouse
- the emotional and financial trauma of divorce
- Finally, visualize yourself getting caught, and the effect this would have on your spouse, your marriage, your children, and your own sense of personal ethics.

For Christine, the whole picture came slowly, an image at a time. One night, lying in bed next to her husband, she thought of all the experiences she and Dan had shared, experiences that Nick knew nothing about. Like the time, just after Sean was born, when the doctor suspected their son had brain damage. She and Dan had been there for each other, through all the scary tests and prayer-filled nights. In the end, Sean was pronounced healthy, and Christine and Dan shared a bond that hadn't been there before.

She remembered the year she put on all that weight—forty pounds. Dan's affection never waned, and Christine had managed to work her way back down the scale. But she had to wonder. Would Nick still be attracted to her if she were forty pounds heavier?

One night she woke up sweating, a scream trapped in her throat. She sat straight up in the dark, feeling frantically for Dan's body next to hers. She felt a shoulder, then heard the pattern of slow breathing. She shuddered at the dark side of her thoughts that had come to life in her nightmares.

She had dreamed about Nick. In her dream they had been standing together in the living room, looking out the window, while she watched as Dan was gunned down by a sniper. The ambulance came, and the police. In a matter of minutes, Christine was a widow. Nick wrapped his arms around her and tried to quell her sobs. But his manner was that of a friend, not a lover. Suddenly another woman appeared in the dream—Nick's wife. Together, Nick and his wife comforted Christine. Then the other couple moved toward the door, leaving Christine alone with grief enough to move a mountain. The message in the dream was clear. Her relationship with Nick was for the moment—it wasn't the stuff of which lives are built together. Her relationship with Dan was the real thing.

And, in her dream, at least, she had managed to lose even that.

Getting out and staying out.

Whether an affair rages only in your mind, or whether your thoughts and his have already paved a path to the bedroom, it's time to get real, get out, and get whole.

No effort is too great, no measure too drastic in the effort to reclaim your heart and recapture wholeness in your life.

These are the steps one woman took as she began to withdraw from an emotional and physical attachment to a young manager at the accounting firm where she worked:

- **Seeing the whole picture:** "The first step, of course, was seeing that Randy and I could never be happy together. I realized that the longer I remained involved with Randy, the greater destruction I would reap for myself, for my husband, and for Randy and his wife."

- **Repentance:** "*Repentance* literally means to turn around. I had to turn around 180 degrees in what I wanted out of my life. My repentance didn't begin with suddenly wanting Randy out of my life, because I still cared for him deeply. Repentance began when I could tell God I was willing for him to *help* me want Randy out of my life. In other words, I couldn't turn around and suddenly become good. But I could turn around and want God to help me want to be good. It was a beginning."

- **Thought-life:** "I banned Randy from my thoughts. Every time I pictured his face, I imagined a big red circle with a slash—like the Ghostbusters' symbol or the 'no smoking' sign—and mentally stamped it across my thoughts. I had to do it maybe twenty, thirty times a day at first. But it worked. Each time I used my 'Randy-buster' symbol, I managed to force him from my thoughts for that moment."

■ **Music:** "I couldn't bear to hear all the romantic, sexy songs on the radio. They just fed my feelings for Randy and my self-pity at having to give him up. I found a Christian radio station and began to feed my mind with lyrics about God and holiness."

■ **Confession:** "I told my husband, Peter, about my feelings for Randy. There were some ugly scenes, but it cleared the air and gave me a sense of accountability. I also told a close friend from church, a woman who is a real prayer warrior. I was really hurting, really grieving over losing Randy. I needed all the support I could get."

■ **Counseling:** "Peter and I found a Christian psychologist and went in for counseling. It didn't necessarily help lessen my feelings for Randy, but it showed me the weak spots in my relationship with Peter, the weak spots that had left me vulnerable to another man."

■ **Prayer:** "I prayed constantly, trying to recapture my old feeling of closeness with God. But it was hard, not because he couldn't forgive me, but because I couldn't accept his forgiveness. I must have wept with repentance before him a dozen times. Then I attended a prayer meeting at a local charismatic church. A woman I barely knew walked right up and said God wanted me to know that he loved me and that he was going to use me to minister to lives around me. I realized at that point that, even though I had spent six months wandering farther and farther away from God, I was only a prayer away from total reunion with him. The parable of the Prodigal Son suddenly took on a whole new meaning."

■ **Total severance:** "Randy and I had already ended our physical relationship, but the emotional ties were strong. It was the hardest decision of my life, but I gave notice and quit my job. I was out of work for a couple of months but finally found a similar position in a firm in the next city."

■ **Recommitment:** "I wanted to recommit to my relationship with Peter, but my feelings weren't coming back full strength for him. I did two things: I began praying that God would restore my love for him, and I began acting and talking as though I were in love again. Sort of an act of faith, I guess. I forced myself to do special things for him like I once had, and I found positive things to say about him when we were together or even with other people. These actions, coupled with my prayers, began to bear fruit."

Two months into her relationship with Nick, Christine began to find her own way out of the mire that had claimed her heart.

On April 17, Christine asked to be transferred to another ward within her hospital, one in which she would rarely cross paths with Dr. Nicholson. The personnel administrator thought the transfer would be approved within two weeks. Christine told Nick the relationship was over. There was pain, but also relief.

On April 18, Christine had a long talk with Dan—about Nick. Dan was relieved that Christine's physical relationship with Nick had ended with a few stolen kisses, but he was visibly shaken by the news. He admitted that their marriage hadn't felt right, not for a long time. He and Christine agreed to see their pastor for counseling and to begin rebuilding their relationship.

On April 30, Christine began her new assignment in post-op.

That afternoon she packed the kids off to her sister's home and picked up a candle and a bottle of sparkling apple cider at the local supermarket. She wanted that evening to be special—a new beginning for Dan and her. The coming months might be tough as she and Dan worked to rebuild intimacy and trust, but she was ready to begin making the investment where it counted—in her marriage.

She was two blocks from home when she turned the car around and drove across town to the shopping mall. She parked and hurried across the parking lot, trying to remember the exact location of the place she wanted to go.

If she remembered right, there was this little boutique, right next to the auto shop, that carried the prettiest, laciest lingerie. . . .

Inflation has hit us all, but an ounce of prevention is *still* worth a pound of cure.

Getting involved is easy.

Getting back out can be a long, painful process for everyone involved.

The very best option is simply to avoid entanglements from the beginning. Linda and I interviewed several Christian leaders regarding illicit relationships . . . and how to prevent them. Here are excerpts from our experts:

Dr. Norm Wright, psychologist and author, had these insights to share:

> "Some people I've seen in my office have literally said, 'I never thought it would happen to me.' And before they tell me the story, quite often I can list: 'It started with this, and this, and this. . . .' They just sit there with their mouths open.
>
> "There is no perfect safeguard for any marriage. When a person says, 'Everything's fine at home,' or 'I don't need to worry about it, I'm safe,' those are danger signals. You always have to be on guard.
>
> "When there's no real bonding in the marital relationship a person is much more vulnerable and prone to have an affair. I have actually told some husbands and wives in counseling, 'You are setting your spouse up for an affair. Of course, he (or she) is ultimately responsible for what he does with the lack of fulfillment in your marriage, but you are really contributing by the way you are responding (or not responding).'
>
> "I'm working with a minister right now who got somewhat involved with a woman in his church. One of his assignments in therapy is to come up with a list of fifteen responses in case this woman approaches him again. And he's rehearsing these out loud to his wife.
>
> "When I am approached romantically by the women I counsel I share with my wife, Joyce, for two reasons: one, as a safeguard, and two, so she's fully aware. Many times office involvement has an edge of excitement about it because there is a forbidden aspect.

When something is brought out into the open, a lot of the excitement evaporates.

"If there are several single working women in a church, they should form an accountability group where they could develop close relationships with each other. Then, when concerns like these arise, the women will gain support from that group. This is imperative because single women don't have the safe-guard of being able to go home to a relationship, or of discussing the situation with a spouse, or of having the accountability that goes along with marriage.

"Someone who is a 'pleaser' can really be taken advantage of. Pleasers don't want to offend anyone; they don't want conflict; they've never learned how to say no. Manuel J. Smith, in his book *When I Say No, I Feel Guilty*, discusses the 'broken record technique.' Let me give an example of what the broken record technique is: You go shopping for a car, and the pushy salesperson comes up and wants to sell something to you. All you have to do is say, 'No thanks. I'm just not interested right now.' Regardless of how much that other person pressures you, as long as you say, 'No thanks. I'm just not interested right now' (even if you say it four or five times), there's no way they can control you. A pleaser is very prone to give a reason. And when you give anyone a reason, you've just handed them control on a platter. I've seen radical changes in people's lives because the broken record, firmly saying no approach gives them a handle on what to do when faced with some of these pressures."

Dr. Ralph Ricco, psychologist, shared these thoughts:

"I believe strongly in accountability. A dear, lovely woman approached me some time ago, and said she wanted me to know what she was going through. She needed someone with whom to be accountable. All of us can be vulnerable—all of us. And when someone says, 'It will never happen to me,' that's the most vulnerable time.

"People get in trouble when they enter a fantasy world. As they continually dwell on something, it does become a reality; that thought will come out in some form.

"So what do I advise? Avoid marriage talk. It can start innocently. You're just conversing, and someone says, 'I like flowers.' You can respond, 'Oh? I like flowers, too.' Or, 'Your favorite vacation spot is the beach? Oh gosh, mine too.' When the topics start becoming a little more intimate—marriage talk—that's a definite red flag. Before long you're comparing spouses, or talking about, 'What if *we* were married?' Or someone might say, 'Why don't we take a picnic lunch to the beach someday? My spouse is out of town.' And then you're in trouble."

Finally, Sylvia Nash, Director of CMA, suggested these preventive measures for today's working women:

"I think we women need to be very careful how we dress, very careful with the kinds of shoes we wear, the kinds of perfume we buy. When we purchase garments to wear to the office, we should take care to dress *professionally*. I have a policy for myself and my staff that it's off-limits to dress seductively.

"There's a lot of 'touch-feely' in Christian organizations, and I'm a hugger myself, so I don't have problems with hugging people—until I realize that it was taken wrong. Then I am careful not to touch that person again. Christians, in general, are always concerned for one another. If we see someone hurting, it's normal for us to empathize with them. A lot of times that opens the door for 'Wow, he's a lot more caring than my husband is' or 'She's a lot more appealing because she's always dressed more beautifully than my wife, who I see in her housecoat every morning, and in her sweats at night.'

"Gordon MacDonald, well-known author and speaker, was asked some years ago, 'If Satan were to attack you somewhere, where would he attack you?' Gordon answered, 'I've never been asked that question. What a strange question.' And the interviewer said, 'Well, give me an answer. What do you think? In what one area of your life could Satan get in there and get you?' Gordon replied, 'Well, I'll tell you one area he wouldn't get me, and that's in my marriage. I have the healthiest and most wonderful marriage, and my wife, Gail, and I are deliriously happy.' One year later he had an affair, in the very area he claimed safeguarded. He and Gail have since rebuilt their marriage. The experience has left its scars but has also brought new depth to their ministry.

"We think, *It could never happen to me*. And then all of a sudden Satan says, 'Oh yeah?' Satan is alive and well, so we'd better wake up. We *are* vulnerable.

"If a manager notices that two members of the team, a male and female, are working late for a number of evenings, that's a big signal. They're very vulnerable; they're getting tired. All of a sudden, they decide they're going to go out and eat together. And they let their guard down. Another red-flag area would be for coworkers; a man and a woman, to do a lot of traveling together. A smart company manager would add a third member on the trip. A company shouldn't ignore the possibilities of affairs happening. Instead, they should make some strict rules to abide by in order to guard against this kind of thing.

"Even little things make a difference. Like, for instance, a secretary taking dictation from her boss. Too many closed-door sessions can lead to problems. Often when I'm meeting in my office with a gentleman I'll leave the door open. It's my way of making this message clear, especially to someone I don't know very well: 'I'm not sure of your motive, but I'm very sure of my motive.'

"Women are gifted with great intuitiveness. So if you sense that a man is interested in something you're not interested in, be smart. Go with your intuition. Don't ever squelch it—even if nothing has happened to give you anything concrete to base it on."

The measures aren't very complicated. Summed up—along with a couple added by Linda and myself—they are as follows:

- Arrange accountability to friends or to a spouse *before* a problem arises.
- Verbally practice saying no long before the opportunity arises.
- Avoid fantasies about off-limits relationships.
- Avoid frequent time alone with any male coworker.
- Respect your intuition.
- Avoid intimate or "What if . . . " conversations with male friends.

- Practice the broken record technique.
- Seek professional help for obvious voids in your marriage.
- Maintain a vibrant relationship with God.
- Above all, recognize that *no one* is immune to an affair—stay on guard.

The preventive measures don't sound difficult, yet they're worth their weight in gold, because the wounds resulting from a few unguarded moments can cut deep. They impact innocent loved ones, as well as the guilty lovers.

And sometimes they never quite heal.

Notes

1. "Do Kids Need a Stay-at-Home Mom?" *Redbook* magazine survey results (August 1986).

2. Peter Kreitler, *Affair Prevention* (New York: MacMillan, 1981), p. 16.

3. H. Norman Wright, *Seasons of a Marriage* (Ventura, Calif.: Regal Books, 1983), p. 6.

4. Kreitler, p. 43.

14

Women and Power

Carving Your Niche
in the Office Power Structure

We can say things are equal, but they're not.
And when we're caught in the crossfire of a battle this hot,
we're bound to get burned sooner or later.

Melita still remembers the day the shrapnel flew. She was sitting in a booth at the only coffee shop within walking distance from the bank. She was eating alone, savoring a tuna on wheat and basking in her most recent achievement.

She had just been promoted to senior loan officer, and it felt good. Years of effort were finally paying off—in salary, in recognition, in a personal sense of reward for a job well done.

"More coffee, ma'am?"

Melita's thoughts scattered and she glanced up at the matronly waitress in orthopedic shoes. "Oh, sure, why not. Warm it up."

As the waitress left the check and turned to leave, something caught Melita's eye. Two officers from the bank were sitting at a table not far behind Melita's. She watched them for a moment,

225

looking for an opportunity to greet her colleagues. But neither man saw her, and she turned back to her lunch.

She was sipping her coffee when something slipped into her ear—just a phrase, really—something about a promotion at the office. But it was accompanied by a low chortle, and Melita choked on an overwhelming sense of dread. She pushed a blue-black lock of hair behind one ear and tilted her head.

". . . senile, anyway," one of the men behind her was saying. "He's probably soft on a pretty face."

"Or a nice set of curves," the other man agreed. "But . . . naw." There was a pause. "You really think so?"

"She's divorced, you know. With a daughter. She probably doesn't get it anywhere else."

"I dunno, Bill. She's been with the bank awhile. Before I came, even. Maybe she deserved it. Maybe it was just her time."

Bill laughed. "Time? Or should we say wine? A little wine, a little song, and bam! She's got the promotion."

Melita's face burned. Her hands shook as she picked up the check and her purse. She took a long drink of cooling ice water, then dabbed a little on her cheeks with one finger. But her face still tingled as hot tears rose to her eyes. She squeezed her lids shut and bit down on her lower lip, trying to regain control.

Five minutes later she slid from the booth. Check in hand, she walked toward their table. The men, talking interest rates now, didn't see her until she was close enough to touch.

"Hello, gentlemen," she said as coolly as she could manage. "I hope you're enjoying your lunch. And be sure to try the wine here. It's excellent."

The matronly waitress, passing by with a bottle of ketchup, slowed to peer at Melita. "Oh, honey, we don't serve wine here," she commented.

Melita turned back toward her colleagues. Bill looked as if he'd swallowed something that was still moving. Melita forced a smile. "I'm sure these gentlemen know that," she said. Then she turned and headed toward the cashier.

She was crying by the time she hit the sidewalk.

Women and power? The combination raises eyebrows and hackles in far too many environments. Men simply have the power edge. It may not be fair, but it's reality.

"A man doesn't have to do a thing to gain power and authority," Sylvia Nash explained in her office during a Monday morning interview. "Society has given power and authority to tall men in particular, and to men in general. But a woman has a lot of work to do, for a lot of years."

She added, "If women are going to get ahead, they have to do *better* than men. If a company is choosing between a man and a woman equal in all professional respects, they're going to choose the man."

As she spoke, my thoughts flashed back to the afternoon I got the rejection phone call about a writing job I'd wanted. I had spent several hours interviewing with my potential boss, and had felt good about our rapport and confident of my skills. Frankly, I was shocked at the news.

"We've decided to hire someone else," the voice on the phone announced.

"Oh. Well. I see," I said politely. I didn't see at all, but there's not too much you can say at moments like this.

"It was neck-and-neck, Karen," the voice explained. "We had a tough time deciding between the two of you. To be quite honest, if you asked me why we hired this other man instead of you, I couldn't even give a reason. But we just did."

My interview with Sylvia Nash shed new light on the power gap between men and women. Magazine articles, books, and statistics all point to the same imbalance:

■ Financially, women earn an average of sixty-four cents for every dollar received by men.

■ In numerous corporations, advancement for women stops at what many are calling the "invisible ceiling." Women, like Melita, who manage to break the barrier and ascend into top management often discover that life can be brutal in the upper echelon, and that credit for a legitimate rise in rank may be hard to come by.

■ The overtime game that seems necessary in the office power struggle is skewed against mothers—married or single—who still retain the primary responsibility for their children.

■ Women who do attain career power may have to sacrifice unduly to get it. Two-thirds of professional women in their forties are childless. Yet 90 percent of their male colleagues have children.

The inequities abound. So how do women handle the challenge of attaining and maintaining power in the workplace?

There's bad news—and there's good news.

Let's get the bad news out of the way first. We'll begin by looking at how women *shouldn't* handle the imbalance.

With the power odds against us,
women are scrambling for
footholds in the corporate climb.
Some sweat it to the top. Others may settle
for a shortcut now and then.

"Sex is power," Robyn complained. It was Friday night, and she and Jason were driving home from a movie.

"You got that right." Jason braked for a red light. "What time is it? Do we have time for pie, or do we have a limit on the baby sitter?"

Robyn held her wrist so the glow from the street lamp hit her watch. "Ten forty-five. We've got time. Baker's Square?"

"How about Polly's?"

Robyn agreed. The light changed and Jason eased the car into the right lane to turn onto the next street. Robyn twisted in the seat to face her husband. "Well? No comment?"

"About the sex thing?"

Robyn nodded.

Jason shrugged. "I agree with you, Robyn. I'm just not surprised, that's all. I see it all the time in sales. Women using a little flirt to close a deal. The smooth-taking guy with the perennial wink racking up major volume with the female purchasing agents. But I guess it's all new to you, isn't it?"

"New? *New?* Jason, I've been homemaking for eleven years. The last time I wiggled my C-cup to get what I wanted, I was a sophomore in high school."

"You wore a C in high school?"

"Jason! I'm serious. It makes me angry. Really angry."

"So, does Bookman listen to her?"

Robyn nodded. "Hangs onto her every word. You can tell when she wants something. She gets this pouty look. And you should see her clothes. Slit up to here and down to there."

"Oh, yeah?"

"Jason, I've heard of successful women being falsely accused of sleeping around, and that's inexcusable. And tragic! But so is this. This woman isn't having an affair with anyone or anything like that, but she sure plays up the fact that she's a woman. She pulls stuff that *seems* harmless, like a little pout here or a wiggle there. She'll flash some cleavage or put on this helpless charade. But it's really detrimental. Here I'm trying to do a *real* job—get taken seriously—and she comes along and disproves everything I'm trying to prove in the office."

Jason pulled into the parking lot at Polly's Pies. "Well, what can you do? She's obviously not too concerned about advancement for women."

Robyn rolled her eyes. "Ah, but she claims she is. She talks all the time about women's rights and stuff. Even has a hyphen in her last name. But when it comes to getting what she wants in the office, she pulls out all the stops."

Sexuality in the workplace can translate into a lot of things. It might result in gender stereotypes, or sexual harassment, or even extramarital affairs. It can also result in illegitimate power garnered by a man or woman who can't—or won't—amass power by appropriate methods.

There aren't any rules on what kind of people tend to use gender power to manipulate friends and influence people. *Every* man and woman needs to be aware of mixed messages, including nonverbal signals, they might be sending to colleagues.

They say all is fair in love and war—and office politics can be full-on war at times. But when either gender turns on the charm to manipulate colleagues of the opposite sex, it introduces a dynamic that is, at best, expedient. The long-range effects—in the lives of individuals as well as in the larger scheme of male/female office relationships—can be downright destructive.

> Just as there are illegitimate
> ways to amass power,
> there are destructive ways to wield it.
> This holds true for men, but it may be
> especially relevant for women.

Just as some women gain power or advancement using less than ethical means, others are hard-pressed when it comes to handling power once it's theirs. We've all met women who seem to feel they have something to prove with tyrannical leadership. According to psychologist Ralph Ricco, it probably stems from a lack of peer acceptance in the workplace. But that doesn't make it any easier to live with. The fact is, some women in leadership never leave home without a chip on their shoulder.

"Let's face it," Ralph told Linda during an interview at his Ventura office, "it's not exactly glamorous out there in the work world. And women can be pretty aggressive. They want to do well, to gain the acceptance and respect not readily granted to women competing in a man's world, which is why some women will go to any means to get a hit. As a result, there can be a lot of infighting, jealousy, pettiness—a dog-eat-dog environment."

Sylvia Nash says women have a disadvantage when it comes to managing power. "Men generally feel more comfortable with power because they've had that role since they were old enough to play in the sandbox," she explained. "Boys have been taught to be the leaders. As a result, they often have a better handle on the use of power as adults.

"For most women, being in a position of power is a new thing. Some women have a tendency to misuse that power and become tyrants. All of a sudden, they have power and they're going to dominate. They're not being passed the baton, but they're taking up the torch. They're not out to lead; they're out to avenge."

She added, "Women need to be very careful about the power given to them, that they receive it with gentleness and administer it with gentleness. Women and men in leadership need to remember we are servant-leaders; we are not 'up here' with all of our servants below. Instead, we are at the bottom, supporting the team that's above us."

While some women misuse their hard-earned power, other women grow resentful as they try to administer that power as though they were men.

Traditionally, there have been few women in leadership. Instead, men have served as the models and mentors for women rising through the corporate ranks.

It's no wonder many women have tried to divorce themselves from perceived feminine traits—including sensitivity, intuition, compassion, affection, and gentleness—resorting instead to perceived masculine traits such as dominance, independence, self-reliance.

Remember Ann's colleague in chapter 2? During an emotion-laden strategy meeting, this woman broke into tears, then apologized profusely for the display of sensitivity, denigrating her coping mechanism as something she'd been raised to do "as a woman." Other women have resorted to dressing like men, or managing a staff as they think a man would do it, intentionally dropping their feminine traits by the wayside. Talk about feeling segmented!

But here comes the good news. Women *can* carve a place for themselves in the corporate power structure, and it doesn't require any of the three destructive approaches discussed above: it doesn't take playing up the fact that we wear a skirt; it doesn't take wielding our power like a battle-axe; and it certainly doesn't necessitate leaving our feminine qualities at home.

The first step toward the successful care and feeding of healthy leadership: Recognizing power traits as gender neutral.

Ann and I talked as I helped her wallpaper the nursery. (I don't usually have to work that hard to get an interview for a book, but, hey, what's a little buying of information between friends?)

Ann handed sopping rolls up the stepladder while I tried not to drip all over the carpet, mismatch seams, or fall and break my neck. In my free time, I quizzed her about the skills that had garnered her promotions, paychecks, and praise in the working world before she made the decision to stay home for diaper duties.

"I didn't do anything different from what I'd done most of my life." She shrugged. "I've always been pretty aggressive, independent, strong-willed. Fortunately, it worked well in my job, which was a major relief."

"Relief? Why was it such a relief?" I asked from under a strip of dripping paper, trying to hold the middle against the wall as the upper half fell about my head. (I had my own version of relief right at the moment; relief would be getting on the phone and calling Al's Paper Hanging.)

"I guess as a kid I never fit the image of the feminine, darling girl," Ann admitted. "I was a tomboy. I chewed my nails; I started my own neighborhood businesses; I was the instigator behind all the parties; I spoke my mind. And I didn't let my dates win at Ping-Pong!"

"I tried that once," I confessed.

"And?"

"And he never asked me out again."

Ann smiled and handed up another paste-sopped roll of paper. "Once my mom, trying to help me attract a boyfriend in junior high, advised me to eat alone in the cafeteria and act helpless, thinking maybe this guy would come join me."

"Did it work?" I asked.

"No."

"Did you even try?"

"No. I mean, I would have felt stupid. I felt bad enough that I didn't act very feminine to begin with. Putting on this big feminine act would have reminded me how badly I was doing in the natural."

The roll of paper in place, I swung one leg around the stepladder and straddled the top step. "Why did you think you were such a failure as a kid?" I peered down at my friend. "Why couldn't all the things you described—aggressiveness, independence, a strong will—be okay for a girl? I mean, those are great traits, the kind of stuff that got you to the top in your field. But you obviously felt it wasn't okay for you to be that way—for a *girl* to be that way."

Ann laughed. "Didn't we grow up in the same generation? C'mon, *you* were there. You know what it was like. It *wasn't* okay. It just wasn't."

"But okay for the guys?"

"Sure. It's always been okay for the guys."

No wonder women can resort to the wrong methods when it comes to choosing and using professional power; the general consensus is that all the really good techniques have already been assigned to the men.

But have they?

Sylvia Nash defines leadership traits as gender neutral: "Leadership is honesty, integrity, being men and women of their word. It is walking tall; it is looking people in the face; it is feeling confident about yourself. These characteristics of leadership would go across the board either way. They're not necessarily male dominant, but they are the qualities anyone, male or female, should strive to possess."

Unfortunately, while many people would pay lip service to her definition, long-standing stereotypes are hard to change.

Harriet Braiker agrees that the solution is to "start thinking in terms of desirable qualities for *people,* and to conceptualize yourself in terms of your personhood rather than your womanhood or femaleness. This is not intended to serve a feminist purpose, but rather the psychological purpose of removing some of the unnecessary murkiness that clouds many women's sense of themselves."[1]

She goes on to add, "There are, in fact, many attributes assigned stereotypically to women that would humanize the business world were they to permeate the political and corporate atmospheres. A little more cheerful, compassionate understanding would help everyone."

In other words, it *is* possible to develop leadership skills *without* resorting to a unisex approach to our jobs. Women—and men—bring unique personal qualities to their professional lives. Many of these qualities are, indeed, gender related.

Sylvia told me about one approach she uses that allows her the freedom to retain feminine traits while diffusing any sense that she's manipulating male peers: "It's a fact that women generally cry easier than men; they have a greater freedom to express their emotions. I have been in situations, in board meetings for example, where I'm facing a very emotionally explosive issue, and I run the risk of crying. At these moments, I open my statements by saying, 'This is an extremely emotional issue for me, and I may cry. But I want you to know that if I do cry, it's not in any way intended to manipulate you, but is simply because this is an extremely emotional issue for me.' Two or three times I have cried. But because I set the parameters at the beginning, I haven't negatively impacted my colleagues. They understand the reason for the crying is not to manipulate them."

Another typically feminine trait that deserves a place in the boardroom is intuition. A recent headline in *Working Mother* magazine read: "Intuition Pays Off on the Job."[2] In another instance, espousing a revolutionary approach to the traditionally bottom-line science of management, Dr. Weston Angor's *Intuitive Management* takes a new look at the old mystery of intuition.[3]

Our unique qualities as women shouldn't be exploited. Neither should they be dismissed.

There *is* a balance, and it's one that's good for women as well as for the companies for which they work.

The second and third steps toward successful care and feeding of healthy leadership: A professional image and a professional work ethic.

One study showed that employees whose managers or supervisors keep their jackets on are 48 percent more productive than counterparts whose leaders opt for the more casual look.[4]

Admittedly, jackets and blazers are not appropriate attire for every profession. But where a jacket is appropriate, Sylvia believes it is a power symbol that neither men nor women can afford to leave at home.

She remembers attending a gathering during which forty Christian leaders met with then presidential candidate George Bush in Washington, D.C. "It was about 104 degrees in the room, and no air conditioner, in the heat of June. And all these men started taking their jackets off. I thought to myself, *I will faint. I will faint and swelter before I take my jacket off.* Because of the power that society automatically awards men, a man can remove a jacket and get by with it. A woman can't."

We've all been warned we can't judge a book by its cover, yet the fact remains that we always try—and sometimes we're even successful. First impressions last a long, long time, and dressing for success is an important step that career-bound women can't afford to overlook.

The third step toward achieving healthy leadership is recognizing the fact that power demands performance. While Sylvia admitted there's probably an equal lack of professionalism among men and women, she said women can't afford to be "just equal" in their quality of performance. After all, being "equal" isn't enough when men still have a power edge based on their gender.

"Women need to shape up," she added. "We need to get our act together. We need to act like leaders before we can be given the leadership power. Women need to volunteer to do projects that are going to demonstrate their leadership. And if we volunteer, we'd better do the right things, like getting the project in on time, having it perfect, having it excellent. When organizations are looking for leaders, they're looking for people who have already proven themselves."

It all boils down to this: If women are going to get ahead, we have to do *better* than men—which may not be as unlikely as it sounds.

Statistics show that women are about 47 percent more productive on the job than men. As Sylvia says, "They're harder workers. I've challenged these statistics with men, asking, 'Do you believe it?' And every man has admitted, 'Yeah, I believe it.' Women are less likely to take a two-hour lunch to chat about the management concerns in the organization. Women work through their lunch. Women are far more conscious about arriving at a designated time. Women are quicker and more efficient in their work productivity. I've really enjoyed asking men about this subject. And to date, I haven't heard anyone say they don't agree."

This phenomenon might be the natural result of being efficient enough to squeeze two full-time jobs—one that pays in dollars and one that pays in love—into the same twenty-four-hour day. It may also be a result of the long-range planning and attention to detail that running a household—with or without the distraction of an outside job—demands.

Teryl Zarnow, family columnist for the *Orange County Register*, wrote in one of her columns: "If you want to get a job done, ask the woman. In most cases she is the one who has ordered school pictures, collected for the paper drive, and organized her day around the soccer schedule. If it is something she cannot do, she will see that her husband does it."[5]

The point is this: Women have transferable home-management skills, as well as skills learned at the office, which can give us the performance edge we need.

But we have to believe it ourselves before we can expect to gain recognition from our peers. We have to recognize that leadership skills are neither feminine nor masculine. We have to dress the part we want to play. And we need to perform to the best of our ability, meeting—and even exceeding—professional standards.

The fourth and final step to making the most of your power potential: Set a realistic course in light of where you are in life.

As Ann and I plastered the final strip of wallpaper in the nursery, she told me how she'd felt the men in her agency had a gender advantage, but it was an advantage that she could combat by being every inch as professional and productive as they were.

But men have a second advantage, and it's a hard one to beat.

Men have wives.

Women don't.

It's a logistical advantage that frees male employees from the majority of child care, laundry, grocery shopping, menu planning, trips to the pediatrician, potty training, Christmas shopping, birthday planning, holiday cooking, back-to-school shopping, parent/teacher meetings, late nights with fevered children, taxi duties, ordering school pictures, joining scholastic book clubs, analyzing junior-high fashion trends, and evaluating the harmful long-range effects of giving in to your preschooler's request for Teenage Mutant Ninja Turtles.

'It's not fair, but it's reality.

It's true that working women all over America are, on a recurring basis, initiating impassioned discussions with their husbands regarding the pursuit of equity of responsibilities on the home front. (Husbands have a simpler definition for the process: They call it "nagging.")

Yet change is a slow process. Even though surveys—like one published in the February 1993 issue of *Working Woman*—indicate that a growing segment of men are beginning to place a higher priority on family life, the fact remains that the bulk of home and child care, in the majority of two-income families, remains the responsibility of the woman. This means that the men in your office—whether they have wives working outside the home or staying home full-time—probably have energy, personal time, and available overtime hours that we only dream about.

Judy Stewart tells a story from her days as a seminary student. On the first day of one of her classes, the professor announced that all of the papers for the course had to be typed. The class was filled with male students, except for Judy. One of the young men groaned. "That's not fair," he complained. "I don't have a wife who'll type my papers." At that point Judy raised her hand and quipped, "Neither do I!"

The "wife advantage" goes far beyond the simple act of typing papers.

As Judy goes on to explain, "For generations, rules in the workplace have been men's rules, which have included workaholism, placing job before family, and reams of overtime. These are the things that have kept corporate America running the way it has for a long time. Men have been free—totally free— to go about the business world and give 99 percent of their time and energy to that field, knowing full well that their wife is at home taking care of everything else."

Linda and I asked Norm Wright about this kind of inequity in the workplace, and whether women can successfully compete against that kind of advantage.

He had a good answer—something about comparing apples and oranges.

"At some level, it comes back to just doing the best you're capable of doing, and not always comparing your progress to that of the person next to you. You have children at home; you can't work overtime. Someone else doesn't have kids— or the responsibility of their kids—so they can work twenty hours a day."

As Linda has observed, that can be a hard pill to swallow, especially for single mothers who have no fewer breadwinning burdens than the married men in their offices. In many cases, single mothers have a greater financial responsibility because theirs is the *only* income for the family, while many men have paycheck-earning wives.

Yet life has never been fair. Some people have more to offer in the looks department. Others are stronger or smarter. Many enjoy circumstances that allow them to be richer. The circumstances of still others allow them to be more educated, while some people enjoy arrangements that allow them to sell extra time or energy to their employers.

Maybe finding success in the crazy world in which we live requires two important skills, the first of which is doing the best with the things we can control. This means constructively changing ourselves, our workplaces, and society where we have the power to do so. It means developing our God-given potential. It also means making sure the pursuit of power has left us uncompromised in our relationships with God, our families, ourselves, and those around us.

The second skill is simply accepting the things we cannot change. After going to work on all the inequities we have a shot at changing, let's trust God with everything that's left. Let's learn to set professional and personal standards based on our own unique circumstances, and not on the circumstances of others; based on our own strengths and potentials, and not on the strengths of people around us.

Maximize your potential, while accepting your limits. There's power in those seven words. No matter what happens on the corporate climb, if you can master these two little principles, you'll accomplish more and enjoy a fuller life than the vast majority of women—and men—in this generation or any other.

Notes

1. Harriet Braiker, *The Type E Woman* (New York: Nal Penguin, Inc., 1986), p. 90.

2. Barbara Berg, "Intuition Pays Off on the Job," *Working Mother* (October 1988), pp. 25-26.

3. Weston Angor, *Intuitive Management* (New York: Nal Penguin, Inc. 1984).

4. Interview with Sylvia Nash.

5. Teryl Zarnow, "No One Gives Mom a Pat on the Back, But Dad Gets Praise," *Orange County Register* (November 9, 1989). Teryl Zarnow is the author of *Husband Is the Past Tense of Daddy*, and is working on a forthcoming book about families.

The way I see it, I'm doing you a favor. I'm saving
you hundreds a year in gym membership fees.

15

"Do You Work?"

Calling a Truce between Stay-at-Home Mothers and Mothers Employed

Ladies and Gentlemen!
In corner number one, wearing a business suit
and two-inch pumps, we have . . . Superwoman!
And in corner number two, wearing stretch pants
and a Gerber-stained sweatshirt, we have . . . Wonder Mother!

It didn't used to be like this.

Once upon a time mothers weren't separated by the yawning chasm created by a simple slip of paper that says, "Pay to the order of . . . "

At one point in time, women actually supported each other.

A long, *long* time ago, women spent more time with each other than they did with their husbands. Women drew water together, washed clothes together, quilted together, canned tomatoes together. They passed child-rearing advice from generation to generation. Time-honored remedies for the croup and teething were the stuff of life. The men of those days were survivalists and hard workers; communication, relating, and marriage enrichment weren't subjects found on any man's list of favorites. And so the women drew together, not just to share the work, but to share an encouraging word and a little understanding.

Even in more recent generations, the bonds of women's networking held strong. Most women stayed home and raised children, their daytime hours peopled with other mothers and other children from around the neighborhood. Grandmothers often lived nearby, offering insights and wisdom from generations past. There was a flow, a sense of personal history, and a sense of gender history as well. It was a time when women felt they had a sisterhood of sorts.

Sounds a little corny now, doesn't it? Probably because the word is so far from describing the way womanhood feels today.

Today women aren't united. We're divided. We're separate. We're alone.

Some say it's because families today are more mobile. Friendships are left behind with the dark square on the linoleum where the refrigerator once stood. Couples that, twenty years ago, might have lived half an hour from their parents now live half a dozen states away.

Some say it's because more families are broken. Relationships with members of our families—people our age as well as older and younger generations—shift like the sands as divorce and separation redefine families and family ties. Continuity and networking among women are lost in the couple-shuffle.

For full-time mothers and other women at home, the neighborhood is a lonely place with most of the other women commuting to a desk or factory somewhere, and all the kids in day care.

And for women balancing a career and family, the pace of life is too harried to spend much time exploring ties with women friends.

Finally, there's the romantic balderdash that says we don't need friends to feel fulfilled; all we need is a single, solitary figure on a white horse, carrying a red rose, waxing eloquent with sweet words. Find him, marry him, and live happily ever after, experiencing nary another need nor problem as long as ye both shall live.

However we look at it, one thing is clear:

The networks between women are broken.

Women feel isolated—and worse.

We feel misunderstood—and even attacked—by members of our own sex.

Anita Shreve, author of *Remaking Motherhood,* calls the division between working moms and stay-at-home moms "very harsh."

The battle line is drawn.

And women of all ages are choosing sides.

**If you thought the bullets flew
in the war between the sexes,
you can imagine what it's like being nailed
by a member of your own army!**

Christine rushed home from work, changed out of her nurse's uniform, and launched right into preparing dinner. She wanted the evening to go perfectly. In three hours, she and Dan would entertain guests; the new associate pastor and his wife were coming to dinner.

Dan arrived home in time to help get the three boys washed and dressed. At six-thirty the doorbell rang. Dan ushered Sam and Jeaneatte Stanley into the living room and over toward the couch. Christine introduced the boys while Dan served soft drinks to their guests.

Jeaneatte Stanley cooed over baby Paulie. "He must be a handful," she said. "We've got two daughters, in second and fourth grade. They say kids'll keep you young."

Christine smiled wryly. "Or bring on the gray!"

Jeaneatte nodded admiringly. "And three boys! What a lively, full household! You must stay pretty busy."

"Oh, yeah," Christine confirmed. "Especially between them and work."

"Oh, you work?" Jeaneatte's voice cooled three degrees.

"I'm a nurse."

"Is that part-time?" Jeaneatte asked politely.

"No, full. I'm off at three, so it works well with the older boys' schedules. And Paulie's at a great day care between here and the hospital."

Jeaneatte winced. "It must be hard leaving the little one. Is he adjusting okay, or is it pretty traumatic for him?"

Christine felt herself stiffen. "Actually, he seems to enjoy the interaction."

Jeaneatte shook her head. "Poor little thing."

"I take it you don't work," Christine said flatly.

"Oh, no! Sam and I decided that our children should be the first priority. I quit work when Evie was born and haven't gone back since. I just couldn't see the sense of it. I mean, if I was going to work, why have children at all?"

We've all felt the barbs. We've all sensed the subtle—and not-so-subtle—accusations. Even Linda—as a single career woman and mother—has her share of war stories to tell. Recently, for example, Linda was invited to attend a women's retreat as one of the featured speakers. Retreat coordinators asked her to address the challenges of managing a home and a career. Yet during her address, a remarkable thing happened: the women were so enthused and impassioned about the topic that the hour turned into more of a discussion group than a lecture.

That evening, the director of the retreat approached Linda and asked if she would conduct a similar session some Saturday for women in the church who had not been able to attend the retreat. Linda agreed, and the director promised to call in the following weeks and set up the event.

The woman never called. Months later, Linda heard from a friend who attends the church. This friend had heard about Linda's retreat session, and she knew the reason why a repeat performance had never been scheduled. It seems that while the majority of women had received tremendous benefit from Linda's address, several homemakers had been offended. They felt that Linda was too "liberated" for their tastes.

It's easy to laugh or shake our head at the misperceptions of those who judge us quickly. But the arrows fly both ways, don't they? If working mothers are the scapegoats for the problems of the world, then full-time moms have received their share of bad press as well.

In her article "Motherhood's No Snap," Kim Wright Wiley observes:

> We live in a society which insists that flawless motherhood is just within reach. . . . A pleasant concept, but there's one drawback: It isn't true. I was in control of the experience of motherhood for about the first three hours of labor and since then it has become a progressively out-of-control experience for me.
>
> Perhaps the worst thing about this "Motherhood's a Snap" school of thought isn't the guilts, it's that it devalues the job of rearing children. After all, if being a mother is easy to do, it can't be all that important.[1]

249

Being a full-time mother isn't exactly high on the prestige scale these days. Just look at the way homemakers are portrayed in the media. I'm offended by all the TV commercials that imply that the performance of any particular cleaning product composes the highlight of a homemaker's week.

And then there's that awkward silence when a new acquaintance asks a full-time mom, "What do you do?" and her answer doesn't imply the possession of a business card.

I know about these things because when acquaintances ask that inevitable question, I'm never quite sure what to tell them. Some weeks I'm a full-time mom. Some weeks I'm a full-time writer. Most of the time I'm somewhere in between. At least I'm home so I can tell people I work at home. That's always a safe answer.

But unless I tell them I'm a writer—or pump them with questions about *their* jobs—the conversation grinds to a halt. People don't know what to ask me. They aren't quite sure I'm versed in any subject other than kidspeak.

I straddle the fence. Despite my career, I'm a stay-at-home mom a good part of the time. And yet, even *I* fall into the trap of stereotyping stay-at-home moms as uninteresting, single-focused, and ambitionless. When I meet a woman who works full-time at home raising children, a part of me recoils. And for a heartbeat—just a single heartbeat—I find myself wondering how we'll hold an intelligent conversation.

And then I remember what it feels like to be misunderstood as a working mother, or devalued as a full-time mom.

It helps me regain my perspective.

Why are we so judgmental?
Could it be . . .
might we feel . . .
is it possible that we're actually . . .
jealous?

Christine admits that she envies the time full-time mothers get to spend with their kids, yet she's not sure she's cut out for twenty-four-hour-a-day maternal duties. "Despite the guilt I feel over time spent away from my sons, I like my job," she says. "It's actually a nice break from the round-the-clock responsibilities at home. If I were at home all day, I think I'd be pretty bored."

Many full-time moms shun the work force because they believe working mothers shortchange their families. Yet staying home all day with active, inquisitive, and progressively independent children isn't easy, either. Full-time moms can find themselves coveting the professional atmosphere, adult interaction, personal satisfaction, salary, prestige, and strokes enjoyed by women in the workplace.

Maybe we're hostile toward each other because we're jealous.

Then again, maybe we're hostile because we're afraid that what the other side thinks of us holds a grain of truth.

Perhaps working women are afraid they *are* shortchanging their families.

And maybe full-time moms are terrified that they *are* leading lives out of the mainstream of society.

Maybe—just maybe—we'll all feel better if we learn to appreciate our differences and support each other anyway.

There *is* no easy path.

Speaking as one straddling the fence, the grass on either side can be pretty parched at times. Full-time moms *and* mothers employed make sacrifices unique to their situations.

There's a chance that, as the trends continue toward "parent" tracks and even sequencing, the chasm between women will narrow. As more women find creative alternatives to the choices between family and career, maybe career and full-time motherhood won't be such an either/or situation. Until that happens, here are a few ideas to help narrow the rift between working mothers and mothers at home.

Perhaps full-time mothers should keep in mind that:

■ **Just because a woman works doesn't make her a neglectful mother.** Many stay-at-home moms spend no more time than their working counterparts in daily one-on-one interaction with their kids. Without subscribing to the myth that *quality* time can displace *quantity* time, the numbers still tell us that, in terms of quality time, many working moms and many full-time moms aren't so different in what they're offering their children.

■ **At-home mothers can become so caught up in volunteer work that they spend little more time at home than their salary-earning counterparts.** There is disparity in the philosophy that says a mother up to her eyebrows in volunteer church work is a better mother than the woman who accepts a paycheck for her efforts. Maybe we should stop drawing the battle line at the paycheck and start evaluating each situation, each decision, and each family—single *and* dual income—on its own merits.

■ **Studies show that the best parents are happy parents.** Most experts agree that young children are best left in the care of their parents, but school-aged children of a happily employed woman are very likely better off than the school-aged children of a woman who feels miserably trapped at home.

At the same time, there are a few concepts that we working moms might find helpful to keep in mind:

■ **Most at-home mothers work as hard as we do**—and for no money, less praise, and fewer days off. Despite the nonstop pace of a working mother's life, the change in environment from home to work provides a respite, which full-time mothers rarely get.

■ **Working moms *need* full-time moms.** These are the room mothers, PTA presidents, scout leaders, and den mothers who contribute to the lives of our children.

■ **Full-time mothers deserve our respect.** Full-time child rearing is a noble challenge, and one that increasing numbers of women from all walks of life are pursuing. Regarding the devaluing of a mother's work, one writer has observed: "Having a family was once considered a big deal for a woman, her life's work, and even though men have never acknowledged the effort that goes into motherhood, other women realized that raising children and raising them well took every shred of intellect and energy that a person could muster. It was a respectable job, one in which the work was acknowledged to be hard, but the rewards were incomparable. The rewards are still incomparable and the work is still hard, and a pox on anyone who says it isn't."[2]

The rift between women didn't develop overnight. Bridging the chasm may be a long process. Women on both sides of the gulf are hurting, nursing wounds inflicted by members of the other camp. And yet it's worth the effort to reach across the gap and befriend someone on the other side. Despite our different lifestyles, we have a lot to teach each other, and more than a lot to learn.

After all, wholeness goes beyond the wholeness of one woman, or even the wholeness within a single family. If we dare to reclaim wholeness between women—women alike in heart despite disparity in choices—all will be the richer for it.

Notes

1. Kim Wright Wiley, "Motherhood's No Snap," *Working Mother* (October 1988).

2. Ibid.

16

Tomorrow's Grown-ups

*Preparing our Sons and Daughters
for the Choices in Their Future*

If our mothers had only known . . .

There are a lot of things our mothers didn't know as we were growing up. For instance, my mom never knew about the time my sister Renee nailed our neighbor Mr. Wilson between the bifocals with a mudball.

On a larger scale, our mothers never had an inkling about the transitions and challenges we would face as women of the 1990s. How could they? The past twenty years have held more changes—in technology, information, values, lifestyles, gender roles, and family units—than occurred during the previous hundred.

Our mothers might have prepared us better—if only they had known. But they didn't. Because when we were growing up, the pace of change and progress was slower. Time was slower. Parents thought our lives and opportunities wouldn't be all that different from theirs.

Surprise!

We're the women who grew up on fairy tales—*before* they were denounced as sexist and unrealistic.

We grew up in an era when couples had 2.5 kids and celebrated wedding anniversaries with double digits. Today we're dating and marrying at a time when traditional two-parent families are under siege, sex can kill, and couples have a better chance of winning the lottery than staying married past their mid-life crises.

We grew up thinking we would be moms, or maybe nurses, secretaries, teachers, or librarians. Today women are all these things . . . as well as doctors, lawyers, mail carriers, CEOs, senators, and astronauts.

We grew up in a time when sex was hush-hush and Coke was something from a wavy bottle. Today eleven-year-olds can get abortions without their parents' knowledge, two million Americans carry the AIDS virus, and our kids can get their hands on crack cocaine more easily than they can obtain a prescription bottle of fluoride tablets.

I've got a weird hunch. My hunch is that society progresses at about the same speed as the current trend in transportation:

- The rate of travel by horse was pleasantly improved upon with the distribution of the first automobiles.
- These were improved upon by newer models.
- Planes brought faster travel yet.

All this progression took place over a matter of centuries. While change came at an increasingly faster pace, lifestyles absorbed the transitions and generations managed to keep up with the shifts. Then, suddenly . . .

Hold on to your faces! We just blasted into hyper-space, folks. We're hauling light-years here. At the rate things are changing, most of the issues we're dealing with today may well be obsolete by the time our kids are grown.

So how do we prepare them for their future?

Unlocking gender stereotypes for our kids.

Kaitlyn and I were in Lucky's supermarket, wheeling past the cut-flower display. From her perch in the shopping cart, she announced: "Boys don't get flowers."

At last count, we've had this discussion twenty-three times.

"Kaitlyn, it's *okay* for boys to get flowers," I responded as if on cue, my delivery about as fresh as the three-day-old flowers supporting each other in buckets of green, tepid water.

"Nope. Boys don't get flowers. Only girls."

I sighed. "Girls may get flowers more *often* than boys do, but it's okay for boys to like flowers and for girls to like trucks, and for boys to play with Barbies and for girls to . . ."

I stopped and scratched my head. Okay for girls to . . . *what?* I'd been trying to help Kaitlyn think beyond gender stereotypes for so long, I couldn't remember what came next.

Not that it works, anyway. Kaitlyn hates her overalls, demands to wear dresses and party shoes every chance she gets, and can't stand a crumb on her face or a blotch on her clothes. She loves makeup and jewelry—*my* makeup and jewelry. But she does have a briefcase.

Okay, okay, so it's a *pink* briefcase, but it's still a briefcase.

The point is, I have no idea how to effectively prepare her for what womanhood—and gender roles—might be like by the time she's nearing her adult years.

Right now, ask her what she wants to be when she grows up, and she'll tell you she wants to be a mom. While that's flattering, I'd like to teach her that she has the potential—and will very likely have the opportunity—to attain any level of professional status she's willing to pursue. Yet, by that process, I don't want to unintentionally devalue full-time motherhood. It remains, after all, a rewarding life-work that contributes to individuals and to humanity in a way no other calling can ever come close to.

And while we're at it, what about our boys? How do we prepare *them*?

Linda says she worries about raising two sons in a single-parent home. Among other things, she worries about the number of household chores Dallas—and Chris, when he was still living at home—have been required to handle because she works. Yet Norm Wright, during an interview at his home in southern California, applauded the very cross-gender training that Linda feared.

One day, he pointed out, our sons may be the husbands of working wives. Literacy in home and child care can only prepare them for the kinds of challenges they're bound to face. And one day they may become the colleagues, subordinates, or managers of working women. Helping them understand family-care issues can only enhance the work environment as well as male/female relationships in the twenty-first century.

Maybe the key is to make no assumptions about the way our kids will spend their lives. I mean, we can no longer raise a daughter ignorant of investment options or her own personal earning power, assuming she'll have—or want—the financial protection of a hard-working husband all her adult life. Nor can we raise a son devoid of household skills, assuming he'll marry the homemaker of his dreams.

We can't discourage a girl from developing marketable skills, assuming she'll never work to feed her family or her self-esteem. Nor can we raise a boy to honor the workaholic career standards his dad and granddad may have followed, assuming he'll be satisfied to sacrifice the rich rewards of a well-rounded life.

And by all means, let's not teach our daughters they can "have it all and have it now"—which would assume they wouldn't mind making the same mistake we started to make with our lives.

Know the facts and count the costs.

Christine realized the family was in trouble as Christmas drew near.

"Drew near" is a relative term, of course. Christmas really wasn't drawing near in terms of calendar months—by *that* measure Christmas was nearly a sixth of a year away.

Christmas was drawing near, however, in terms of marketing power. It was the first week in November, and already Sean and Justin had watched 3007 toy commercials featuring Santa Claus, snowflakes, or reindeer, as well as 1,499 subliminal messages that read: "Obtain this toy at any cost—Repeat: *Any cost!*—which includes being placed for adoption by harassed and irate parents."

The cumulative impact was beginning to take hold. The boys had already tacked Christmas lists to the refrigerator door. (Christine had to lift the lists to *find* the refrigerator door.)

Christine complained about the problem one night to Dan. He was tinkering under the hood of their car as it sat parked in their garage. Christine had pulled up a paint-stained stool and watched her husband as he worked.

"Dan, the boys don't seem to realize there are *costs* attached to these things," she groaned.

"Maybe we spoil 'em." Dan's voice was muffled, his face buried somewhere in the engine.

Christine screwed up her face in thought. "Do we?"

Dan straightened up and peered at his wife from around the hood. His smudged face made him look like a raccoon. "You tell me. It seems to me we work pretty hard to make life easy for them."

"You really think so?"

"Honey, with you working we buy them things we never would have thought of buying before—brand-name clothes, toys, sports equipment, special events like that rafting trip with the school, summer camp, the Disneyland thing. They get almost whatever they want. And they want a lot."

Christine sighed. "You might be right."

"Did Sean ever help you with the dishes tonight?" Dan quizzed.

"Well, not really." Christine's voice sped up as she hurried to explain. "There were just a few and I decided to go ahead . . ."

"See what I mean?" Dan wagged a grimy finger at Christine. "We're soft on the boys, Chris. We cover for them too often. They think the world is theirs for the asking. You're right. They *don't* understand the costs. And no wonder! We haven't taught them any differently."

Understanding the costs of requests, of decisions, of privilege—what a novel idea!

Wouldn't it be great if we could raise children fully aware of the fact that *any* path they take in life will require a price? If we could teach them to evaluate the costs and returns in light of godly values and biblical standards?

In chapter 12 we quoted psychologist Pamela Addison on the cost of dropping her practice to quarter-time in order to raise her daughter, Melissa. Pamela had this to say about the cost of combining an aggressive career with small children at home: "If I'm going to choose to take the promotion and my kids are going to be in day care, then I have to know what the limitations of that are going to be, and what effect it's all going to have on our family life. Nothing comes easy. It isn't easy or comfortable for a woman to have a career and a family and to do both things well; there's a compromise on either side. Whichever choices you make, you just need to be thoughtful about what you're choosing and what you're giving up."

I admit that I went into marriage unaware of the cost of my decision. I had subscribed to this attractive idea that, once I married, all my problems would be over. In fact, I've come to the conclusion that I didn't really marry my husband, Larry. I married a warm body onto which I could project my image of the Prince Charming who had been destined before birth to fulfill my every emotional, sexual, intellectual, and social need.

Needless to say, my fairy-tale marriage demanded more than a few rewrites.

A couple of years ago, I finally realized what I had done and took a long, hard look—past the hologram image I had projected onto my husband, to the man himself. He was rather different from the person I had thought I married.

I was actually pretty shocked. Even more so when I realized that the task before me was to discard the image and to get to know and learn to love the real man. For a period of time I wasn't happy about the matter.

I mean, having to face *reality*? Good night!

Once I got past the newness of the idea, however, it was actually refreshing. Freeing even. Sure, I had to learn to live with a few quirks and foibles. I had to learn the art of compromise. And I had to let go of some of my rather idealistic expectations. But these adjustments were considerably less draining than the impossible task I'd been struggling with for years, which was to force a flesh-and-blood man into the shape and form of an intangible, projected image.

My story has a happy ending. But not every story does. Every day, men and women are swept into circumstances they never took the time to fully understand, and the end results can be tragic.

Cults, for example, are identified in part by the fact that members aren't given full details about the group's strangest beliefs or activities until *after* they've made the decision to join. At that point, members find themselves immersed without warning in a harsh, controlling environment, often isolated from outside friends and family and subjected to rituals and beliefs they *never* would have considered if they had only known.

In abortion clinics across the nation, young women are misled about the costs of their decision. They go to the tables and the knives believing that the process will be easy—that it will be brief and painless; that it is safer than childbirth; that there will be no life-threatening complications; that they can conceive again whenever they want; that there will be no psychological impact; that they will never regret their choice, never cry on the anniversary of their baby's death, never wake in the middle of the night mourning an empty womb and empty arms. For them, the awakening into reality is more bloody, more harsh and hellish than mine ever came close to being.

Linda and I have a passion to see the next generation of young men understand the full ramifications of having a working wife—before they marry one. The benefits include financial security and the opportunity for men to focus on the joys of family life. The costs include accepting equal responsibility on the home front so that wives can chart a manageable course in life.

We have a desire that tomorrow's women understand the special joys that come with full-time mothering—that in their eyes the role of a stay-at-home mother is not devalued, but granted all of the prestige and respect that it deserves. At the same time, our daughters need to understand the costs of making the choice to raise children at home. Staying home—happily—means accepting less recognition; accepting that you may never catch up with the careers of friends who chose a different path; accepting that there will be moments when you feel out of the mainstream of society.

Finally, we have a burning desire that women who choose to combine family life and a career would do so, being well-informed. Realistic expectations are essential, as well as the ability to say no, a commitment to keep family first, and a willingness to dream big, work hard, and live full.

Freedom from traditional roles requires a tighter grip on biblical values.

We're sending our kids into the unknown.

Unfortunately, there's no way we can anticipate—and prepare them for—every choice they'll have to make in the course of their lifetime.

Their lifestyle may end up much, much different from ours. We'll have to learn to cope with that, just as many of our parents learned to cope as our lives took a path different from theirs.

But some things aren't optional. Linda and I believe these things are: a godly character, a commitment to biblical values, and a personal relationship with Jesus Christ. In the wild waters of a rushing, changing tide, our children will need to know there is a Rock on which to stand; that Rock is God.

As gender identity and the very texture of family life are shaken like willows in the wind, reshaped and redefined by a society in the throes of change, our children will need to know that their identity and worth in Jesus Christ remain untouched.

As we make our way in a world where resources and even people are misused, abused, and discarded, our children will need to know how to be good stewards of the gifts of their skills and the even richer gifts of marriage, parenthood, and friendship.

And as men and women wallow in a heady potion of the power derived from the things of the world, our children need to know the power of God's Word, the power of his Spirit, the power of prayer, and the power of godly living.

Linda and I agree that there are few passages in the Bible that speak so eloquently to hearts facing the unknown as Psalm 139. Let it remind us—and remind our families—that there's nothing on this earth we face alone:

> O Lord, you have searched me and you
>   know me.
> You know when I sit and when I rise;
> you perceive my thoughts from afar.
> You discern my going out and my lying down;
> you are familiar with all my ways.
> Before a word is on my tongue you know it
>   completely, O Lord.
> You hem me in—behind and before; you have
>   laid your hand upon me.
> Such knowledge is too wonderful for me, too
>   lofty for me to attain.
> Where can I go from your Spirit?
> Where can I flee from your presence?
> For you created my inmost being; you knit me
>   together in my mother's womb.

My frame was not hidden from you when I was
    made in the secret place.
When I was woven together in the depths of
    the earth,
Your eyes saw my unformed body.
All the days ordained for me were written in
    your book before one of them came to be.
How precious to me are your thoughts, O God!
How vast is the sum of them!
Were I to count them, they would outnumber the
    grains of sand.
When I awake, I am still with you.
Psalm 139:1-7, 13, 15-18, NIV

17

Living Full in Each Season of Your Life

Working Women Need to Have It All

I got the phone call while watching the end of some made-for-TV movie: Ann had gone into labor. Since Larry wasn't home yet from teaching an evening class, I debated. Should I? Naw, there was always tomorrow. Then again . . .

In the end, I bundled Kaitlyn in a blanket, grabbed my Thomas Guide map, and headed toward the hospital, half an hour away, where Ann, Rick, and other friends and family had already congregated. Kaitlyn chatted drowsily as we sped down the freeway. I parked the car as close to the hospital entrance as possible, hefted my six-year-old into my arms, and scurried across the lot.

Ann's parents were there, as was another couple I didn't know. Ten minutes after I arrived, Robyn and Jason showed up after getting their neighbor to sit with their two girls. There was no news yet about the baby.

As the clock ticked and the men watched local news on the waiting room TV, Ann's mother chatted with Robyn and me. Before long the other woman—who introduced herself as

Rick's sister—joined us as well. We shared—what else?—stories from our own childbirth hours.

Remember, in chapter 15, I said that sisterhood among women is dead? Well, there's one exception. One milestone can kindle a bond and an empathy between women regardless of age or job status. That milestone is childbirth. Women who have experienced it nod knowingly while hearing the details of another mother's ordeal and blessing. Women who aren't yet mothers listen with dread and anticipation to the strange tales of the unequaled privilege and unsurpassed pain of childbirth.

At a quarter to twelve the double doors at the end of the corridor swung wide. Rick emerged, grinning. We flocked to his side, shouting questions. He waved a hand to lower the noise level. Raising his own voice to overcome ours, he said simply, "Boy!"

A cheer went through the group. A nurse, passing on the left, held one finger to her lips. Robyn reminded us to hold it down.

Rick informed us we could enter the ABC room in groups of two and spend a brief moment with the new baby and mother. I waited till the others had their turn, then asked Robyn and Jason to hang around an extra few minutes to watch Kaitlyn, who had fallen soundly asleep on one of the couches in the waiting lounge.

Rick stood outside the door, talking excitedly with Ann's parents. I brushed past him into the room.

Ann was trying to nurse Bryan Michael, who nosed blindly around her breast, mewing like a kitten. His mottled red skin looked paper-thin and fragile as he grasped Ann's forefinger with five translucent fingers of his own. His eyes were closed, and his tiny mouth searched for the nipple. When he found it, he suckled for a moment and then turned away to begin his search again.

Ann smiled. "He doesn't have the hang of it yet."

I drew closer, enchanted by the tiny features of life perfect. "He will," I said softly.

"What a miracle, huh?" Ann asked.

I nodded. "And you? How are you?"

"Numb. Exhausted. Relieved. Exhilarated. I feel like I got run over by a truck, and I'm ecstatic at the same time."

"Oh, yeah. I remember that combination."

"I can't imagine missing out on this," Ann mused, staring into the face of her son.

"Missing out? How could you miss out?" I asked. "For centuries women have *tried* to miss out on labor and delivery. No one's bypassed it yet."

"I don't mean that. Sure, *that* part's a little rough—" she said.

"A *little?*" I winced. "That's the entire reason they tell you to pick a focal point other than the face of your labor coach. When you go berserk from pain, fly off the handle, and look for something to throttle the snot out of, it's best not to be looking directly at your husband."

Ann laughed. "I'm serious!"

"Okay, okay." I surrendered. "So what do you mean, 'missing out'? You said you couldn't imagine missing out."

"Oh, Karen, you know how hard it was for me to give up my career."

"Temporarily," I reminded. "You're 'sequencing,' remember?"

Ann nodded. "Right. Sequencing. I'll go back one day, we both know that. But it's hard. I still feel like I'm missing out on a little something—a few career years that I may or may not be able to make up. A little momentum delayed or even lost forever."

"That's possible."

"The point is, I can live with that decision," Ann added passionately. "I can live with sacrificing 10, maybe 20 or even 50 percent of a great career. But what if I had missed out on *this?"* Ann nodded down at Bryan, sleeping now against the warmth of her skin. "Not the labor and delivery part," she added, "but the relationship part, with him and with Brittney and even with Rick. What if I hadn't made the decision to take the time for *them?"*

"I understand," I said quietly.

"Taking time for the miracle of family—and having a career that's a little less than what it might have been—it's still rich, Karen. It's still rich."

"Richer than choosing career all the way?" I asked.

"For me? And for most of the women I can think of? Yes. The answer is yes."

What Ann was telling me wasn't a new concept. I remembered reading a passage in which Harriet Braiker wrote about the differences in the way women and men define success.

Generally speaking, men consider themselves "successful" if they garner achievements in the arenas of work, money, and professional status. That means "career all the way" can fit in with many men's concept of success. Even as a wealthy man mourns failed relationships with women or with children, he may still consider himself a successful person.[1]

But it's a rare woman who, finding recognition in the business realm but a void or failure in her personal life, defines herself as "successful." For women in the marketplace, success *must* encompass the personal life as well as the professional . . . the home life and the work life.

Next question: Is that even possible? After all, following years of practice, even men haven't managed to perfect that feat!

Linda and I have come to the conclusion that, for generations, men have *looked* as if they've "had it all." They've given a great impression of being able to balance all the balls in the air at once. Marriages, children, and breakneck careers have appeared pretty compatible—at least from a distance.

But we know better, don't we?

We've all heard the horror stories of "successful" men who neglected their wives and never knew their children. We've read about the divorces—at least the famous ones—splashed in newsprint and across magazine covers. And every night on shows like "Geraldo" and "Sally Jessy Raphael" we can hear the bitter accusations of the children who grew up and turned to substance abuse or crime or violence or sex; looking back to the birth of their great emotional void, too many point fingers back at dads who were never there for them.

After all these years, we're discovering the guys *haven't* had it all, after all. But what they've had, for many men and for many centuries, has seemed for them *almost* enough. At least enough for many men to point to accumulated wealth and status and power and claim, "I've made the mark. I have . . . success."

But women don't have that option. If we're going to make our mark in the workplace—and if we're going to feel good about ourselves as we're doing it—we may *have* to have it all. Because for us, success is defined differently, and relationships with loved ones aren't elements that we can sacrifice easily to the gods of commerce.

At least not if we intend to live with ourselves afterward.

Working women can have it all, but maybe not all at the same time.

Last week I got a card from Melita. The postmark read Gary, Indiana.

The last time I saw her was several months ago, when she dropped by to return a stack of books she'd borrowed half an eon ago. She had unearthed them in the process of packing. She and Brenda had made their decision: They were moving to the Midwest.

I remember she told me life had come to a place of choices. An either/or fork in the road. A matter of priorities.

"I mean, we can go on living in California," she had explained, "and have great weather, great friends, more stress, less spendable income, and little time for each other. Or we can take a leap of faith, move to the Midwest and have awful weather, make new friends, live a slower pace, pay less rent, and have more time for each other."

"Sounds like either choice comes with its share of sacrifice," I commented.

She nodded. "The question wasn't *whether* we should sacrifice, but *what* we should sacrifice for our family at this time in our lives."

Nobody keeps their cake and eats it, too. Sacrifices abound for men and women at every age and every stage of life.

Robyn had to choose between staying home full-time or spending more time with her husband. She chose Jason—but working full-time meant sacrificing in other areas as Robyn found herself struggling to release expectations and standards she had lived with for years.

Christine chose between the thrill of romance with Nick and the satisfaction of a lifetime love with Dan.

Ann decided her job was too demanding for her family at that stage in their lives. She weighed the cost and made a sacrifice that made sense for her and for the people she loved.

Melita's choice meant taking the risk of changing jobs and moving to a more affordable part of the country, but in return she got financial freedom and more time with Brenda.

When Jenny decided to stay home with Mathew, it meant giving up the salary, adult interaction, and positive strokes that had accompanied her full-time job. Later, as financial needs demanded, she found a way to sacrifice some freedom and free time to bring in money—without sacrificing her commitment to home-care for Mathew.

I remember a conversation with Jenny about the time her baby-sitting business had grown to involve five children.

"So is that okay?" I asked her over the phone. "It's not like you planned all this; it just sort of happened. Are you happy about it?"

The line fell silent a moment as she thought about her answer. "It's not what I want to do with the rest of my life, if that's what you mean. But for now, yeah. It's good. It's good for us financially; it's good for the friends I'm helping when I watch their kids. And it's good for Mathew, because I'm home."

"But for the future . . ."

"Nothing against the kids I watch—they're great. But I'll be honest with you. This isn't the long-term plan for my life."

And therein lies the opportunity to have it all . . . do it all . . . be it all.

Time.

Time brings new landscapes against which our decisions take on new colors. The hues and shapes making up our lives one year from now may be incredibly different from the picture we live with today.

It's easy to feel that life will never change, that our families will remain locked in today's circumstances, pressures, and challenges forever.

Yet few things remain untouched by the hand of time. Beauty fades. Relationships grow or die. Financial burdens shift. Incomes rise or fall. Children mature. Sickness comes and goes. Economies fluctuate. The health of friends and family may weaken or thrive. Sometimes death comes, as do births. Families find themselves in new homes, in new cities, in new regions of the country. Bosses quit or transfer. Careers skyrocket or stagnate.

The choices we make for ourselves and our families today may not be necessary or even appropriate tomorrow. A sacrifice made today may be returned to us threefold tomorrow.

Over the course of a lifetime—accepting accomplishments in stages and respecting the sacrifices demanded by each stage—maybe, just maybe, we *can* have it all.

Learning to live with imbalance— because the perfectly balanced life may not be the best fodder for greatness.

I opened the door to our home office and stuck my head in. "Larry, the contractor's here."

Larry set aside the bills he was paying and joined us in the kitchen. Ronnie Alexander, sitting at the table, had already inspected our house and was ready to give us his quote to rebuild our roof.

But first, he flashed us a beaming grin from the top of his six-feet, four-inch frame and waved a work-worn hand, signaling us to take seats. With the other hand he produced a portable cassette recorder. "Where can I plug this in?" he asked, eyes dancing. I gestured to an outlet behind him.

"I'll just take a minute of your time," he explained, jabbing the power cord toward the outlet, "but you've got to hear this. I just finished recording this, and I know you're gonna love it."

Larry looked at me, a question mark in his eyes.

"Okay, are you ready?" Ronnie asked, his finger poised above the play button on the recorder. His toes, clad in unlaced, paint-stained Reeboks, tapped against the linoleum in anticipation. "Do you like opera?"

"Opera?" Larry repeated. "Sure, I guess. But Karen and I aren't too familiar—"

"Then you'll appreciate what you're about to hear. Years of work. Years."

He pushed the button and the room filled with the resonance of a richly tenored voice—Ronnie's voice, singing some aria we'd never heard before, in a language we couldn't understand. Ah, but the passion of a soul and the perfected craft of an artist, forged into a single note—*that* we could understand!

Ten minutes later, Ronnie plunged the stop button and told us his dream of becoming a world-class tenor. His remarkable voice was, even then, attracting the attention of many opera greats. In the meantime, Ronnie rebuilt roofs to make a living and pay for voice lessons that cost over one thousand dollars a month. He sang six to ten hours daily, regimenting exercise and even eating habits to enhance the quality of his voice. He kept a tape recorder in the bathroom and in his car so he could work in a few scales around brushing his teeth or between appointments with roofing clients. He even sang on people's rooftops as he manhandled equipment and shingles.

After expounding music for a good twenty minutes, Ronnie got down to business, gave us his quote, and left. As the front door closed behind him, Larry and I slumped against the wall and wondered what had hit us. A whirlwind? The ravings of a madman? A genius?

One thing Ronnie Alexander *wasn't* was balanced.

All my life it seems I've heard the glories of balance extolled from teachers, pastors, summer camp keynoters and nutrition counselors in my high-school health classes. And all my life I've felt guilty because I'm not, well . . . balanced.

If I followed all the advice of balance advocates:

- ■ I would eat religiously from the four food groups three times a day.

- My devotions with God would consist of equal portions of praise, confession, petition, and thanksgiving for prayers answered. (Of course, the petition portion would be divided into progressively smaller segments beginning with petitions for the world, for the missionaries, for my church, for my friends and family, and a few passing requests for myself.)

- The hours I spend sedentary at my computer would be balanced by a series of aerobic activities designed to launch my heart into hyperpulse. And, of course, the pace of every athletic session would conform to a bell-shaped curve, with the appropriate proportions of activities labeled: warm up, cardiac crisis, and cool down.

- My hours with Kaitlyn would reflect a healthy balance of constructive criticism, positive reinforcement, values development, self-esteem building, and physical affirmation.

- And about the division of *my* time, it would have to include pockets of time for a well-balanced array of people spanning age and income brackets, as well as pockets of time for activities including leisure, productive, personal, familial, religious, secular, professional, and recovery.

- All the while, I would be progressing at an equal rate in my emotional, physical, spiritual and psychological development.

And of course, I would repeat the cycle every twenty-four hours!

Let's cut the idealism and get straight to real life. We could spend so much time arranging the logistics of balanced living that we'd never really live a minute of it. A woman juggling a job and a family knows better than anyone that there's hardly enough time in a day to shower and shave your legs at the same time, much less feel satisfied that you've taken care of the needs of the entire world.

Besides, earning success at *anything*—parenting, writing books, growing a marriage, running an office, managing a small staff, teaching Sunday school, disciplining new Christians, cooking, leading a Bible study, running marathons, or singing an aria—demands an imbalanced investment of energy and of time.

It's true. Excellence demands inequity.

Maybe not over the course of a lifetime. Over a period of six or seven decades, there's probably time for almost anything. But on a day-to-day or week-to-week basis, we can't do everything. The issue isn't one of balance, but of priorities.

There simply are times when:

- a major overhaul at Mom's office requires overtime that relegates a family to a month's worth of Stouffers.
- a husband or wife enrolls in graduate school, and life goes on "hold" for a couple of years as the supporting partner holds down a job, proofreads dissertation drafts, and watches TV alone at night while "honey" hits the textbooks 'til dawn.
- a floundering marriage demands emergency attention, prompting a husband and wife to cut work

hours and bypass promotions to invest the hours to save their hearts and home.

- the seemingly sudden appearance of preschoolers in a home requires the full-time attention of one of the parents.
- kids have to adjust as one or both parents work day and night to save a business teetering on the edge of bankruptcy.
- a wife sacrifices momentum in her career while her husband makes a big play in his.
- a husband sacrifices momentum in his career while his wife makes a big play in hers.

The key is to accept imbalance in chunks—and if the imbalance threatens to get out of hand, don't forget where your treasures lie.

Remember Ronnie, the crooning contractor? We developed a fast friendship, and Larry and I watched him pursue and perfect his craft over the coming months and even years. Two years ago, he moved to New York, where his voice has captured the attention of the movers and shakers in the world of opera. Ronnie recently returned from touring Europe and is looking forward to a full schedule of tours and debuts. For Ronnie Alexander, imbalance has been transformed into excellence.

But I still remember a period of months, in the midst of his imbalanced pursuit, when a stepdaughter fell in with a dangerous high-school crowd. As she teetered on the brink of crisis, Ronnie's music fell by the wayside. The tape recorders fell silent as Ronnie and his wife walked their family through a treacherous time. When needs arose, Ronnie knew where his priorities were.

Imbalance equals excellence—but not at the expense of the ones we love.

As we brainstormed on this final chapter, Linda reminded me of Solomon's wisdom in Ecclesiastes, chapter 3. We believe if we had written this famous passage specifically for working women, it might have looked something like this:

There is an appointed time for everything.
And there is a time for every event
    under heaven—
A time to plant, and a time to reap.
A time to strive, and a time to rest.
A time to cook, and a time to create jobs for the
    fast-food industry.
A time to clean the house, and a time to shrug
    and look the other way.
A time to help, and a time to be helped.
A time to give, and a time to take.
A time to seek the praises of a boss,
    and a time to cultivate the love of a child.
A time to strive to meet a deadline,
    and a time to strive to build a family.
A time to go to work, and a time to turn your
    heart toward home.
A time to confront, and a time to give in.
A time to network with your peers,
    and a time to rekindle the fires of a marriage.
A time to earn, and a time to spend.
A time to accumulate, and a time to give away.
A time to minister to friends,
    and a time to evaluate the state of your
    own heart.
A time to say yes, and a time to say no.
A time for material wealth,
    and a time to pursue the greater riches
    of the soul.

Living with—and loving—the seasons of our lives.

I was pregnant with Kaitlyn when I got a bad case of the envies.

It's not a rare side effect of pregnancy (although I had plenty of those). It's simply that I suddenly realized my husband had something I didn't: He had a good forty years to pour into a career. He had a substantial block of time with which to make any kind of professional impact he wanted.

What did *I* have?

I figured I had a few years after college to build up steam in my career . . . and then a dozen or more years of distraction or, worse, total interruption while I bore, breast-fed, and trained small people. After our family was, for the most part, raised—as Larry accepted the presidency of some university or corporation—I envisioned myself scrambling to recapture lost momentum, to regather skills that had begun to stagnate at whatever level I had attained up until that moment when my career came to a screeching halt: the moment they wheeled me out of the delivery room.

I'll admit it. Even as I work nearly full-time from home, there are still days I'm green with envy as I watch Larry back the car out of the driveway and head into work. I mean, he gets to wear real clothes—the kind that are rarely exposed to fingerpaint and Play-Doh. He gets to have real conversations with colleagues and never once has to listen to them whine, "But I don't want to eat it—it looks gross." He even gets to have power lunches in which apple slices and macaroni and cheese do not play the starring roles. And he never, *ever* has to be a room mother for the kindergartners' Valentine's Day party.

Even as we women strive to incorporate men into the ebb and flow of family life, we have to admit that—so far, at least—we have remained the primary movers and shakers on the home front. And while that home front manages to alter the very structure and texture of our days, our husbands seem to emerge relatively unscathed. Sometimes it doesn't seem fair.

Anyway, that's how I feel on the bad days.

Luckily, those days are vastly outnumbered by the good days.

Let me tell you about what they're like.

On the good days I think about spending forty years pursuing the same vision at the same pace under the same stress—and I gag.

I think about the workaholic lifestyle that men are just now beginning to question—and I break into a cold sweat.

I think about a lifetime of work with no maternity leave, no one demanding my skills at painting tiny fingernails, no time off for afternoon baseball games, no one offering me a taste of their frozen Otter Pop, no little person calling my name in the night, and nothing else to distract me from whatever it is I do to earn a buck—and I feel an overwhelming sadness, a gut-sadness that starts down here and works its way throughout my entire being.

And I feel sorry for the guys. Sorry that they've got this block of forty-some years and that, by society's dictate, they still have very few choices about how they're going to spend that time.

It's all so—so *same.*

It reminds me of what it feels like to live in southern California your entire life. Born and raised in Downey, California, I used to think West Coast living had it all—until Larry and I spent two years in the Midwest early in our marriage and I discovered this phenomenon called seasons. At the end of the two years, Larry finished his doctorate, we moved back to California, and I began to realize there was something missing. Our first Christmas back home, I hung our outdoor Christmas lights wearing a T-shirt and shorts. The same Saturday I went Christmas shopping, my husband mowed the lawn.

It's not just that California doesn't have a winter; it doesn't have a fall, either, because the weather doesn't get cold enough to change the colors of the leaves.

I'll admit, one fall I spotted some richly colored leaves. I was in a craft shop and they were selling these plastic bags of fake fall leaves. I bought six bags and sprinkled them on our lawn.

Larry didn't think it was too funny.

The point is, there is something satisfying, rejuvenating, comforting about the seasons of a year—and the seasons of womanhood. The seasons remind me that I play one small part in a bigger picture—that there is a pulse, a sequence, a journey set into motion by the very hand of God himself. The seasons remind me daily of God's timing, of nature, of the ebb and flow of life, of the things that matter.

Finally, the seasons remind me that everything is for an allotted time.

This too shall pass . . .

The good and the bad, the triumphs and trials, the blossoms of springtime and the dark days of winter.

This too shall pass . . .

The joys of small children, the financial stress of a very tough year, the pace and pressure of balancing too many balls in the air at one time.

This too shall pass . . .

And when it's all done—when the cycle of seasons has run its course—how significant it will be to know we saw the value of each and every season of our life; to know we took the time to fully appreciate the short-lived joys of each; and to know we took nothing of value, and no one we loved, for granted in the nonstop march of time and progress.

Face it. We women are in the midst of transition. Our roles are shifting like the ocean tides, even as our opportunities expand toward the heavens. As we wrestle with the changes, we'll probably make more mistakes and accomplish greater things than we ever dreamed possible as kids growing up in the 1950s, 1960s, and 1970s.

Yet it's possible to face the gales of change with a confidence born of inner wholeness. It's possible to negotiate the rapids buoyed by integrity—the integrity that comes from valuing "being" over "doing," relationships over things, people over process. It's even possible to set sail for the horizon itself, pursuing the potential inherent in every season of our lives.

And it's possible to do more than survive. It's possible to *thrive* on the privileges, joys, and challenges that are uniquely ours as women charting new frontiers for ourselves, for our families, and for generations to come.

Note

1. Harriet Braiker, *The Type E Woman* (New York: Nal Penguin, Inc., 1986), p. 4.

**If you work outside your home,
you know it can be a jungle out there.
Then again, life at home
might not seem any tamer!**

The
Working Woman's

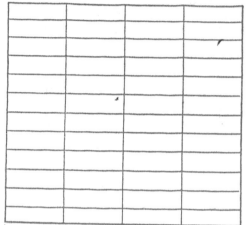
Compil... Guide

...urvival
...ding:

...nselves
...Homes

...rpts ...

Mor...

...daily!

For you...
TX, 75...

...nville,
...olland.